LOOKING AT TYPE SERIES

Looking at Type and Learning Styles

by Gordon Lawrence, Ph.D.

CENTER FOR APPLICATIONS OF PSYCHOLOGICAL TYPE, INC.
GAINESVILLE, FLORIDA

Published by
Center for Applications of Psychological Type, Inc.
2815 NW 13th Street, Suite 401
Gainesville, FL 32609
(352) 375-0160

Looking at Type is a trademark of
Center for Applications of Psychological Type, Inc.
Gainesville, FL.

CAPT, the CAPT logo, Center for Applications of Psychological Type are trademarks of
Center for Applications of Psychological Type, Inc., Gainesville, FL.

Myers-Briggs Type Indicator and MBTI are registered trademarks of Consulting Psychologists
Press, Inc., Palo Alto, CA.

Printed in the United States of America.

ISBN: 0-935652-33-7

Acknowledgements

I would like to express appreciation to the people who contributed knowledge, editorial review, and support during the development and completion of this project, including Charles Martin, Jerry Macdaid, Jamelyn DeLong, Mary Ellen Crenshaw, and Jean Reid. As always, I have been supported in this writing by my wife, Carolyn, and I thank her wholeheartedly. I am also grateful to the more than one hundred people who read the learning style description for their type and provided a critique and wording suggestions.

Contents

INTRODUCTION

This booklet about learning styles is based on the different types of mental processing identified by the Myers-Briggs Type Indicator® (MBTI®). Most likely you have already responded to the MBTI and have received an explanation of your results. If that's true for you, you are probably exploring what the results mean for you in your daily life—including the ways you study and learn. Taking the MBTI is not essential for using this book. To help all readers stay tuned to the basic ideas behind the MBTI, I have included descriptions of the 16 mental-processing types it identifies, as well as other materials. My objectives are the same for all readers: to spark your interest in finding out which of the types is the best fit for you, and to help you examine the strengths, key motivations, and blind spots of your type, as these relate to how you can do your best learning—or teaching, since the book is for teachers as well as students.

The learning styles you will read about here are based on research. In over 200 separate research studies, people were grouped by their MBTI type preferences and were observed in learning situations to see how they chose to learn—what they gave attention to, how they went about learning something, how they solved problems—and how well they did with different kinds of learning tasks. The results of the studies showed very clear learning preferences.

As applied to the types of mental processing, I prefer the term "learning preferences," to the term "learning style" because "style" suggests something on the surface of a person, like a fashion in clothing, which comes and goes and can easily be changed. I use "learning styles" in the book because it is by far the more common term.

The learning preferences shown by the research are deep and not easily changed. In fact, people who teach others about type say that there is no sense in trying to change your type to fit different situations. What makes sense is to use an understanding of your type to decide what learning tools and techniques you can choose that will be the best fit for your type—and give you the best results.

The Learning Preferences

Let's begin by looking at the four sets of learning preferences that go with the MBTI types. Think about the kinds of mental processing that are most natural to you. In the four sets of lists that follow, read each pair of opposite statements on a line and choose a statement from either the right-hand or left-hand column that fits you better.

WHEN LEARNING SOMETHING NEW, I WOULD RATHER:
E   —or—   I

E	I
• Talk out my thoughts as they come to me	• Keep thoughts inside until they're polished
• Plunge in	• Try things out in my thoughts first
• Interact with other people or things while learning	• Do my learning in private, individual ways
• Look around myself for ideas and energy	• Look inside myself for ideas and energy
• Try out ideas right away	• Take plenty of time before I act

WHEN LEARNING SOMETHING NEW, I WOULD PREFER:
S   —or—   N

S	N
• Doing something practical, useful right now	• Doing something that catches my imagination
• Starting with solid facts	• Starting with interesting concepts
• Going step by step in new material	• Finding my own way in new material
• Starting with known things and adding on	• Exploring possibilities
• Starting with first-hand experience that gives practice in things to be learned	• Sampling new skills rather than practicing familiar ones
• Starting with hands-on things	• Starting with a concept or idea

I DO MY BEST LEARNING WITH:
T   —or—   F

T	F
• Teachers who organize the classroom with logical systems	• Teachers who organize the classroom through harmony and personal relations
• Feedback that shows what I do and don't accomplish	• Feedback that shows appreciation of me as a person
• A cool, objective approach to things	• Personal relationships as the key to my learning
• Clear, logical material to study	• Issues and causes I care deeply about
• Things I can analyze	• Situations where helping people is the main work

I GET MY BEST ENERGY FOR LEARNING WHEN I:
J   —or—   P

J	P
• Have things organized in a clear plan	• Can explore things without preplanning
• Have deadlines and stay well ahead of them	• Spontaneously follow my curiosity
• Do my work in a steady way toward completion	• Do my work when the surges of interest take hold of me
• Know just what I am accountable for	• Have genuine choices in assignments
• Have instruction that is organized and moves in predictable ways	• Have work that feels like play

Now go back over your choices. In each of the lists, add the choices on each side, and circle the letter (E or I, S or N, T or F, J or P) above the list that got the most choices. You'll come out with four letters as your preferences. Mine are E, N, T, and P. As you'll see in the next table, these letters stand for extraversion, intuition, thinking, and perception. There are 16 possible combinations. If you have your results from the MBTI, there is a good chance the four letters you got from these lists will match your MBTI letters. If they don't match, don't worry about it. While these lists contain real differences, supported by research, the wording of the lists was not developed through decades of instrument research as was the MBTI.

Four Sets of Preferences

Let's relate the lists of learning preferences to the types identified by the MBTI. The types of mental processing presented here were discovered by Carl Jung, the Swiss pioneer in the field of psychology. He called them psychological types. His work was extended by an American, Isabel Myers, the author of the MBTI. A person's responses to the MBTI are sorted into four pairs of opposites, like the four pairs of lists of learning preferences. In the table "Words to Help Understanding of Type Concepts" the words describe general preferences, not just learning style. The four sets of preferences are extraversion and introversion, sensing and intuition, thinking and feeling, and judgment and perception.

Extraversion and Introversion. Jung invented these terms to mean outward-turning and inward-turning. Everyone has to extravert and introvert every day. We are extraverting when we turn outside ourselves to act, and we are introverting when we turn inside to reflect. We have to have skills in both, but one is our preferred way. It is the way a person gets energized. Extraverts get energy by turning outward to act. Their batteries run down when they are introverting. Introverts get their batteries charged in private reflection, and extraverting drains their energy. Everyone has a preference for one or the other, in much the same way as having a preference for using the right hand or left hand for writing, throwing a ball, etc. It is important to keep in mind that being *skilled* in extraverting is not the same as having a natural *preference* for extraverting (and getting energized by extraverting). I suggest you read the E and I lists in the table and compare them to the E and I lists you responded to earlier. Can you see how they relate to each other?

Sensing and Intuition. Sensing and intuition are two kinds of perception, two different ways of becoming aware. When we use our senses to become aware of people and things, we learn what is actually, concretely there—facts. When we use our intuition to become aware of things and people, we have hunches and see possibilities beyond facts. Using our sensing, we focus on specifics, not the overall picture. Using our intuition, we see the overall picture, with little attention to specifics. Everyone uses sensing and intuition, but prefers one over the other. The preferred one automatically comes into action first, gets used more, and becomes our more confident way of perceiving. The less-preferred one is used as a helper, and does not come into use automatically. Read the S and N lists in the table and compare them to the S and N lists you responded to earlier.

Thinking and Feeling. Thinking and feeling are two ways of making judgments, two ways of reasoning. When we reason with thinking, we are using impersonal logic—reasoning to find a non-personal conclusion and looking for cause-and-effect reasons. When we reason with feeling, we move in close to find how a decision will affect people and things we and others care about. When reasoning with feeling, our decision is based on our priorities among our values, and not on whether it would seem logical to an outside observer. We all need to use thinking judgment for objective reasoning and feeling judgment for reasoning that weighs the effects of the decision on people's feelings and what they care about. Everyone uses both thinking and feeling ways of reasoning, but each of us prefers one over the other, uses it more, and is better at it. That one comes automatically into action, and the other is used in a helper role.

It is important to remember that feeling judgment is not the same as *emotional reaction*. An emotional reaction can decide things, but that is not *reasoning*. Thinking types and feeling types alike can settle things on the basis of emotional response, but they are not being rational when they do. The act of thinking or feeling, as Jung meant it, is rational. Read the T and F lists in the table and compare them with the T and F lists you responded to earlier.

Judgment and Perception. In some people, their judgment preference, thinking or feeling, shows in their outer life, and the letter J is used in the four-letter type description, as in ESFJ and INTJ. In other people, the perception preference, sensing or intuition, shows in their outer life, and the letter P is used, as in ESFP and INTP. The Js, the people who run their outer life with their judgment preference, want to have their outer life planned and running by the plan, settled, decided, and organized. They do their perceiving work—sensing or intuition—quietly and inside where it doesn't show so much to the outer world. The Ps, the people who run their outer life with their perception preference, S or N, want to have their outer life *open* to new perceptions. To them, preplanning sets up barriers to the flow of information they want to get from their senses or intuition. They want to keep plans to a minimum so they can be flexible and respond quickly to new things as they happen. They steer their outer life by making a lot of small adjustments as things go along, as one steers a bike. The Ps do their judgment work—thinking or feeling—quietly and inside where it doesn't show so much in their outer life. Read the J and P lists in the table and compare them with the J and P lists you responded to earlier.

Have you chosen a preference on each of the four dimensions? What is your hypothesis type—your best estimation at this point of the type that is the best fit for you? Read the type descriptions that follow. Start with the description that goes with the four letters you chose.

WORDS TO HELP UNDERSTANDING OF TYPE CONCEPTS

E: EXTRAVERSION

When extraverting, I am . . .
- Oriented to the outer world
- Focusing on people and things
- Active
- Using trial and error with confidence
- Scanning the environment for stimulation

I: INTROVERSION

When introverting, I am . . .
- Oriented to the inner world
- Focusing on ideas, inner impressions
- Reflective
- Considering deeply before acting
- Finding stimulation inwardly

S: SENSING PERCEPTION

When using my sensing I am . . .
- Perceiving with the five senses
- Attending to practical and factual details
- In touch with the physical realities
- Attending to the present moment
- Confining attention to what is said and done
- Seeing "little things" in everyday life
- Attending to step-by-step experience

- Letting "the eyes tell the mind"

N: INTUITIVE PERCEPTION

When using my intuition I am . . .
- Perceiving with memory and associations
- Seeing patterns and meanings
- Seeing possibilities
- Projecting possibilities for the future
- Imagining; "reading between the lines"
- Looking for the big picture
- Having hunches; "ideas out of nowhere"
- Letting "the mind tell the eyes"

T: THINKING JUDGMENT

When reasoning with thinking, I am . . .
- Using logical analysis
- Using impersonal criteria and principles

- Drawing cause and effect relationships
- Being firm-minded
- Prizing logical order
- Being skeptical

F: FEELING JUDGMENT

When reasoning with feeling, I am . . .
- Applying personal priorities
- Weighing human values and motives, my own and others
- Appreciating
- Valuing warmth in relationships
- Prizing harmony
- Being trusting

J: JUDGMENT

When I use my judgment process outwardly, I am . . .
- Using thinking or feeling judgment in my outer world
- Deciding and planning
- Organizing and scheduling
- Controlling and regulating
- Goal oriented
- Wanting closure, even when data are incomplete

P: PERCEPTION

When I use my perception process outwardly, I am . . .
- Using sensing or intuitive perception in my outer world
- Taking in information
- Adapting and changing
- Curious and interested
- Open minded
- Resisting closure to obtain more data

The Sixteen Types of Mental Processing

As you will see, the descriptions that follow were written to represent adults, people who have lived long enough to have developed clear preferences among the mental processes. Some children exhibit the preferences early, others later. As you consider matching descriptions to people you know, I suggest you start with adults at this point, and consider children's types later on.

The descriptions are arranged with opposites across from each other; for example, ENTJ is across from ISFP, the type that is opposite in all four dimensions. As you read the phrases listed for each type, you should *not* assume that a positive value listed for one type implies a negative trait for the opposite type. For example, when we read that ENTJs value efficiency we must not infer that ISFPs are inefficient. Similarly, because ISFPs value compassion does not mean that ENTJs are cold-hearted. Opposite types are across from each other to help you decide your best-fit type. The contrasts shown by the opposites help to clarify what is given priority in our mental processing. What has high priority for ISFPs is not given high priority by ENTJs, and vice versa.

In reading the Descriptions of the Mental-Processing Types, you will notice several things about how the types are presented:

- The descriptions are mostly about what is valued, what is given highest priority, in each of the mental processing types.
- In each of the four-letter type designations, such as ENTJ and ISFP, one of the letters is larger than the others.
- In each of the descriptions, one of the mental processes is said to be strongest, and is described as extraverted or introverted.

These features need some explanations. **What is valued** is emphasized in the descriptions. The type descriptions written by Myers and others, listed in the Resources section, give more emphasis to *behaviors* associated with each of the types—behaviors that represent strengths and likely blind spots. Here the descriptions emphasize the values and priorities that are *motivating energy* lying behind the behaviors. This book being about students' learning styles, our focus is on motivations for learning and how best to tap into them. Each type has a motivation pattern different from the others. Some types are similar, and some are opposite in what they value in their mental processing. The types most different from each other are across the page from each other.

The larger letter in the four-letter type designations, such as ESTJ, refers to the mental process that is strongest, called the dominant mental process. An explanation of this follows the descriptions.

ENTJ

Intuitive, innovative ORGANIZERS; analytical, systematic, confident; push to get action on new ideas and challenges. Having extraverted THINKING as their strongest mental process, they are at their best when they can take charge and set things in logical order. They value

- Analyzing abstract problems, complex situations
- Foresight; pursuing a vision
- Changing, organizing things to fit their vision
- Putting theory into practice, ideas into action
- Working according to a plan and schedule
- Initiating, then delegating
- Efficiency; removing obstacles and confusion
- Probing new possibilities
- Holding self and others to high standards
- Having things settled and closed
- Tough-mindedness, directness, task focus
- Objective principles; fairness, justice
- Assertive, direct action
- Intellectual resourcefulness
- Driving toward broad goals along a logical path
- Designing structures and strategies
- Seeking out logical flaws

ENFJ

Imaginative HARMONIZERS who work well with people; expressive, orderly, opinioned, conscientious; curious about new ideas and possibilities. Having extraverted FEELING as their strongest mental process, they are at their best when responsible for winning people's cooperation through caring insight into their needs. They value

- Having a wide circle of relationships
- Having a positive, enthusiastic view of life
- Seeing subtleties in people and interactions
- Understanding other people's needs and concerns
- An active, energizing social life
- Seeing possibilities in people
- Thorough follow-through on important projects
- Working on several projects at once
- Caring and imaginative problem solving
- Maintaining relationships to make things work
- Shaping organizations to better serve members
- Sociability and responsiveness
- Structured learning in a humane setting
- Caring, compassion, and tactfulness
- Appreciation as the natural means of encouraging improvements

ESTJ

Fact-minded practical ORGANIZERS; assertive, analytical, systematic; push to get things done and working smoothly and efficiently. Having extraverted THINKING as their strongest mental process, they are at their best when they can take charge and set things in logical order. They value

- Results; doing, acting
- Planned, organized work and play
- Common sense practicality
- Consistency; standard procedures
- Concrete, present-day usefulness
- Deciding quickly and logically
- Having things settled and closed
- Rules, objective standards, fairness by the rules
- Task-focused behavior
- Directness, tough-mindedness
- Orderliness, with no loose ends
- Systematic structure; efficiency
- Categorizing aspects of their life
- Scheduling and monitoring
- Protecting what works

ESFJ

Practical HARMONIZERS and workers-with-people; sociable, orderly, opinioned; conscientious, realistic and well tuned to the here and now. Having extraverted FEELING as their strongest mental process, they are at their best when responsible for winning people's cooperation through personal caring and practical help. They value

- An active, sociable life, with many relationships
- A concrete, present-day view of life
- Making daily routines into gracious living
- Staying closely tuned to people they care about so as to maintain harmony
- Talking out problems cooperatively, caringly
- Approaching problems through rules, authority, standard procedures
- Caring, appreciation, compassion and tactfulness
- Helping organizations serve their members well
- Responsiveness to others, and to traditions
- Being prepared and reliable in tangible, daily work
- Loyalty and faithfulness
- Practical skillfulness grounded in experience
- Structured learning in a humane setting

ESTP

REALISTIC ADAPTERS in the world of material things; good natured, easy going; oriented to practical, first-hand experience; highly observant of details of things. Having extraverted SENSING as their strongest mental process, they are at their best when free to act on impulses, responding to concrete problems that need solving. They value

- A life of outward, playful action, in the moment
- Being a troubleshooter
- Finding ways to use the existing system
- Clear, concrete, exact facts
- Knowing the ways mechanical things work
- Being direct, to the point
- Learning through spontaneous, hands-on action
- Practical action, more than words
- Plunging into new adventures
- Responding to practical needs as they arise
- Seeing the expedient thing and acting on it
- Pursuing immediately useful skills
- Finding fun in their work and sparking others to have fun
- Looking for efficient, least-effort solutions
- Being caught up in enthusiasms

ENTP

Inventive, analytical PLANNERS OF CHANGE; enthusiastic and independent; pursue inspiration with impulsive energy; seek to understand and inspire. Having extraverted INTUITION as their strongest mental process, they are at their best when caught up in the enthusiasm of a new project and promoting its benefits. They value

- Conceiving of new things and initiating change
- The surge of inspirations; the pull of emerging possibilities
- Analyzing complexities
- Following their insights, wherever they lead
- Finding meanings behind the facts
- Autonomy, elbow room, openness
- Ingenuity, originality, a fresh perspective
- Mental models and concepts that explain life
- Fair treatment
- Flexibility, adaptability
- Learning through action, variety and discovery
- Exploring theories and meanings behind things
- Improvising, looking for novel ways
- Work made light by inspiration

ESFP

REALISTIC ADAPTERS in human relationships; friendly and easy with people, highly observant of their feelings and needs; oriented to practical, first-hand experience. Having extraverted SENSING as their strongest mental process, they are at their best when free to act on impulses, responding to the needs of the here and now. They value

- An energetic, sociable life, full of friends and fun
- Performing, entertaining, sharing
- Immediately useful skills; practical know-how
- Learning through spontaneous, hands-on action
- Trust and generosity; openness
- Patterning themselves after those they admire
- Concrete, Practical knowledge; resourcefulness
- Caring, kindness, support, appreciation
- Freedom from irrelevant rules
- Handling immediate, practical problems and crises
- Seeing the tangible realities
- Finding least-effort solutions
- Showing and receiving appreciation
- Making the most of the moment; adaptability
- Being caught up in enthusiasms
- Easing and brightening work and play

ENFP

Warmly enthusiastic PLANNERS OF CHANGE; imaginative, individualistic; pursue inspiration with impulsive energy; seek to understand and inspire others. Having extraverted INTUITION as the strongest mental process, they are at their best when caught in the enthusiasm of a project, sparking others to see its benefits. They value

- The surge of inspirations; the pull of emerging possibilities
- A life of variety, people, warm relationships
- Following their insights wherever they lead
- Finding meanings behind the facts
- Creativity, originality, a fresh perspective
- An optimistic, positive, enthusiastic view of life
- Flexibility and openness
- Exploring, devising and trying out new things
- Open ended opportunities and choices
- Freedom from the requirement of being practical
- Learning through action, variety, and discovery
- A belief that any obstacles can be overcome
- A focus on people's potentials
- Brainstorming to solve problems
- Work made light and playful by inspiration

ISFP

Observant, loyal HELPERS; reflective, realistic, empathic, patient with details. Shunning disagreements, they are gentle, reserved and modest. Having introverted FEELING as their strongest mental process, they are at their best when responding to needs of others. They value

- Personal loyalty; having a close, loyal friend
- Finding delight in the moment
- Seeing what needs doing to improve the moment
- Freedom from organizational constraints
- Working individually
- Making peace behind the scenes
- Attentiveness to feelings
- Harmonious, cooperative work settings
- Spontaneous, hands-on exploration
- Gentle, respectful interactions
- Deeply held personal beliefs
- Reserved, reflective behavior
- Practical, useful skills and know-how
- Having their work lives be fully consistent with deeply held values
- Showing and receiving appreciation

ISTP

Practical ANALYZERS; value exactness; more interested in organizing data than situations or people; reflective, cool and curious observers of life. Having introverted THINKING as their strongest mental process, they are at their best when analyzing experience to find the logical order and underlying properties of things. They value

- A reserved outer life
- Having a concrete, present-day view of life
- Clear, exact facts
- Looking for efficient, least-effort solutions based on experience
- Knowing how mechanical things work
- Pursuing interests in depth, such as hobbies
- Collecting things of interest
- Working on problems that respond to detached, sequential analysis and adaptability
- Freedom from organizational constraints
- Independence and self-management
- Spontaneous, hands-on learning experiences
- Having useful technical expertise
- Critical analysis as a means to improving things

INFP

Imaginative, independent HELPERS; reflective, inquisitive, empathic, loyal to ideals: more tuned to possibilities than practicalities. Having introverted FEELING as their strongest mental process, they are at their best when their inner ideals find expression in helping people. They value

- Harmony in the inner life of ideas
- Harmonious work settings; working individually
- Seeing the big picture possibilities
- Creativity; curiosity, exploration
- Helping people find their potential
- Having ample time to reflect on decisions
- Adaptability and openness
- Compassion and caring; attention to feelings
- Work that lets them express their idealism
- Gentle, respectful interactions
- An inner compass; being unique
- Showing appreciation and being appreciated
- Ideas, language and writing
- A close, loyal friend
- Perfecting what is important

INTP

Inquisitive ANALYZERS; reflective, independent, curious; more interested in organizing ideas than situations or people. Having introverted THINKING as their strongest mental process, they are at their best when following their intellectual curiosity, analyzing complexities to find the logical principles underlying them. They value

- A reserved outer life, and an inner life of logical inquiry
- Pursuing their interests in depth, with concentration
- Conceptual skills
- Work and play that is intriguing and not routine
- Being free of emotional issues while working
- Working on problems that respond to detached intuitive analysis and theorizing
- Approaching problems by reframing the obvious
- Complex intellectual mysteries
- Being absorbed in abstract, mental work
- Freedom from organizational constraints
- Independence and nonconformity
- Intellectual quickness, ingenuity, invention
- Competence in the world of ideas
- Spontaneous learning by following curiosity and inspirations

INFJ

People-oriented INNOVATORS of ideas; serious; quietly forceful and persevering; concerned with work that will help the world and inspire others. Having introverted INTUITION as their strongest mental process, they are at their best when caught up in inspiration, envisioning and creating ways to empower self and others to lead more meaningful lives. They value

- A reserved outer life and a spontaneous inner life
- Planning ways to help people improve
- Seeing complexities, hidden meanings
- Understanding other people's needs and concerns
- Imaginative ways of saying things
- Planful, independent, academic learning
- Reading, writing, and imagining
- Being restrained in outward actions; planful
- Aligning their work with their ideals
- Pursuing ideals and clarifying their ideals and core beliefs
- Taking the long view
- Bringing out the best in others through appreciation
- Finding harmonious solutions to problems
- Being inspired and inspiring others

ISFJ

Sympathetic MANAGERS OF FACTS AND DETAILS, concerned with people's welfare; stable, conservative, dependable, painstaking, systematic. Having introverted SENSING as their strongest mental process, they are at their best when called on to use their sensible intelligence and practical skills to help others in tangible ways. They value

- Preserving and enjoying things of proven value
- Steady, sequential work yielding reliable results
- A controlled, orderly outer life
- Patient, persistent attention to basic needs
- Following a sensible path, based on experience
- A rich memory for concrete facts
- Loyalty; strong relationships
- Consistency, familiarity, the tried and true
- Firsthand experience of what is important
- Compassion, kindness, caring
- Working according to a plan and schedule
- Learning through planned, sequential teaching
- Set routines, common sense options
- Rules, authority, set procedures
- Hard work, perseverance

INTJ

Logical, critical, decisive INNOVATORS of ideas; serious, intent, highly independent, concerned with organization; determined and often stubborn. Having introverted INTUITION as their strongest mental process, they are at their best when caught up in inspiration, turning insights into ideas and plans that will improve human knowledge and systems. They value

- A restrained, organized outer life, and a spontaneous, intuitive inner life
- Conceptual skills, theorizing
- Planful, independent, academic learning
- Skepticism; critical analysis; objective principles
- Originality; independence of mind
- Intellectual quickness, ingenuity
- Nonemotional tough-mindedness
- Freedom from interference in projects
- Working according to a plan and schedule
- Seeing complexities, hidden meanings
- Improving things by finding flaws
- Probing new possibilities; taking the long view
- Pursuing a vision; foresight; conceptualizing
- Getting insights to reframe problems

ISTJ

Analytical MANAGERS OF FACTS AND DETAILS; dependable, conservative, systematic, painstaking, decisive, stable. Having introverted SENSING as their strongest mental process, they are at their best when charged with the responsibility of organizing and maintaining data and material important to others and to themselves. They value

- Steady, systematic work that yields reliable results
- A controlled, outer life grounded in the present
- Following a sensible path, based on experience
- Concrete, exact, immediately useful facts and skills
- Consistency, familiarity, the tried and true
- A concrete, present-day view of life
- Working according to a plan and schedule
- Preserving and enjoying things of proven value
- Proven systems, common sense options
- Freedom from emotionality in deciding things
- Skepticism; wanting to read the fine print first
- Learning through planned, sequential instruction
- Immediately useful facts and skills
- Quiet, logical problem solving
- Hard work, perseverance
- Serious and focused work and play

About the type differences. Do the differences on these lists seem real to you? The are very real, and the type preferences are reflected every day in the ways we choose to do our learning. Knowing the strengths, values, and tendencies of your type of mental processing—and using that knowledge in daily life—can help you make the most of your assets.

Teachers reading this may be thinking, "How can I keep 16 different motivation patterns in mind when planning lessons? This is not realistic." You're right; it is not realistic. Farther on, I will be showing you some shortcut ways to use the type differences in your daily work. What is important at this point is to see that the differences are real, and that they are deep and important, not superficial.

The dominant mental process. What does the larger letter mean, as in ESTP or INFJ? When we look at motivation through the lenses of type differences, the most important feature in motivation is what's called the *dominant* mental process. The larger letter identifies the dominant in that type. In Jung's view, *all* mental processing can be sorted into one of four categories— sensing perception (S), intuitive perception (N), thinking judgment (T), and feeling judgment (F). And in each person, one of the four is dominant. It is the process that comes into action automatically and first. It sets the stage for the other three, which assist the dominant. It plays by far the biggest role in the personality. You can see in the type descriptions how important the dominant is.

The mental processes are used in different attitudes or directions. If S, N, T, and F are the mental processes, what are E, I, J, and P? They are the directions, inward or outward, in which S, N, T, and F are used. The E types use their dominant extravertedly—as in ESFP, sensing is dominant and extraverted. Look at the ESFP and ESTP type descriptions—the two types with sensing dominant and extraverted—and you will see sensing in action in the outward direction. The P at the end of the four letters means that a *perception* process, sensing perception in this case, shows in the outward direction and is used in running the outer life of this type. P types want to run their outer life with perceptions open, catching as many new and interesting experiences as possible.

The other two types with sensing dominant, ISTJ and ISFJ, use it introvertedly, where it does not show so much to the outer world. The I types keep their dominant inside for inner mental work. They use their second favorite process—a *judgment* process—in their outer life, as indicated by the J. In ISTJ it is thinking judgment that runs the outer life, and in ISFJ it is feeling judgment that runs the outer life. Both want an orderly, planful outer life, but they use the opposite kinds of judgment to provide the plan and order. Read these two to contrast with ESTP and ESFP. To summarize, extraverts use their dominant in their outer life, introverts reserve the dominant for the inner life. J and P tell whether it is a judgment or perception process that shows outwardly. So for extraverts, the J or P tells their dominant process. For introverts, the J or P tells their second favorite process.

You can use type ideas well without knowing about the dominant and its direction in one's life, but type concepts are richer when you do know. What I have written in these three paragraphs took me a long time to digest and understand. Don't worry if you don't understand them right away.

The Basic Motivations

You will notice in the Descriptions of the Mental-Processing Types that the types with the same dominant mental process are grouped together: thinking and feeling dominant types across from each other in the first four pairs of descriptions, and sensing and intuition dominant types across from each other in the last four pairs of descriptions. The dominant tells us the most about the basic motivations of the types. Let's consider how they show up in classrooms.

The students with **thinking** dominant come to class expecting to find logically organized experiences. They want their teachers and the learning materials to give them opportunities to learn the cause and effect relationships of things, what makes things tick. If they don't find logical reasons and order, objectivity and fairness in the teacher, their main motivation is drained away, and they can't bring their best to their studies.

When students with **feeling** dominant come to the classroom, logical orderliness is not a priority in their minds. They want to find a teacher that cares about students, connects with students with warmth and compassion, and provides learning experiences they can put their heart into. If they find abrasiveness in the classroom, their desire for learning in that classroom shuts down, even if the abrasiveness is not directed toward them personally. They just want to get out.

Key to Motivation: the Dominant Mental Process

To use the ideas of type in making learning more potent, we need to focus on the power of the dominant mental process.

SENSING: When sensing perception is dominant, the key to motivation is having experiences that are—above all else—physically real, useful here and now, and practical.

INTUITION: When intuitive perception is dominant, the key to motivation is having experiences that—above all else—hold fascinating possibilities and engage imagination.

THINKING: When thinking judgment is dominant, the key to motivation is having— above all else—logical orderliness in one's life, either in the inner life of the mind, or in the outer events of one's life. Things need to make sense.

FEELING: When feeling judgment is dominant, the key to motivation is having—above all else—harmonious relationships in one's life.

When the person's dominant mental process is constructively engaged in the task at hand, he or she is open to learning and growing, with all mental resources available.

The students with **sensing** dominant may value a logically-ordered classroom and harmonious relationships, but these are not the main motivations for them. They want, above all else, to have something practical to learn, something clearly useful *right now*. The teacher's expression, "Trust me. Some day you'll be glad you learned this," is a definite turn-off. Unless they see the immediate utility of an idea or skill, and learn its value through practicing using it, they cannot bring their best energy to the work—no matter how much they believe an education is important.

Intuition dominant students may appreciate logical order, friendliness and warmth, and immediate practicality in their classroom, but these are not the keys to their motivation. They must find inspiration there, something that sparks their imaginations, or they will feel wooden and numb, which they hate more than anything in the classroom setting. They will merely go through the motions of learning, or make sparks for themselves by doing something unauthorized, or just find that their minds have gone elsewhere.

Do you find your own reactions to classroom instruction described here? Do you see a connection between your reactions and the dominant mental process you have identified as yours?

The pull of the dominant process in our mental life is very strong. One's mental processing type can be thought of as a set of lenses through which life is experienced. The dominant is the most important lens. In the view of Jung and Myers, a person cannot stand outside of his or her mental processing type. The dominant process always remains in the center of mental activity.

From the standpoint of the teacher, lesson plans should be checked to see that something in them will appeal to S, N, T, and F kinds of motivation. If the plans don't touch all the bases, they risk causing some students to work against their natures to try to learn what is expected.

From the standpoint of the student, there is the problem of what to do when assignments and class work don't fit your kind of mental processing. The question is, "What can I do to make this work appealing and satisfying—to better match the way my mind works?" For Ts: "Can I build a logical system here if the teacher doesn't provide one?" For Fs: "With whom or what can I make a personal bond to get me feeling positive about this work?" For Ss: "How can I make this work tangible and practical enough to put meaning into it for me?" For Ns: "How can I bend this work so that it grabs my imagination?" If you have a teacher who doesn't understand different motivations, the wrong attitude to take is to expect the teacher to take the initiative to fix things for you. You take the initiative. Offer suggestions of what variations of work would help you to learn better. The lists that fill the last part of this book will give you ideas of what learning options to suggest to the teacher.

Ways Of Viewing Type And Learning

Beyond being aware of the power of the dominant mental process in learning situations, there are two practical ways to look at type and learning preferences. One is to look separately at the four pairs of preferences—E and I, S and N, T and F, and J and P—to see what works well for Es that is different from what Is prefer, and so on with all four preference pairs. Most research on type and learning has been done from this viewpoint. We will look at these contrasts first. After that are the tables that show a second way of viewing learning preferences: type by type for all the 16 types—ENTJ, ESTJ, etc.

E and I Differences in Learning: What Works

For *extraverted* students:

- **Small group and partner work** is especially important for extraverts, who do their best thinking when processing thoughts aloud. Introverts don't mind working with someone else so long as they are with a partner they choose. In the classroom, quiet-voice rules should apply: Talk so your voice can be heard just 10 inches away.

- **Sloppy copy** (rough draft writing) **and other trial and error opportunities** fit the extraverts' need to plunge in. Having time to try things out before having to be accountable for them also helps introverts.

- **Physical movement while learning** especially helps extraverts. Along with talking, extraverts need outward-acting. In classrooms, the movements need to be quiet and not bothering other people.

- **Observing others at work**, seeing how competent adults (and other students) do their work, including mental work, is an example of the extraverts' looking outside themselves for ideas and values. This is another part of learning by interacting.

- **Making learning products to be used by someone else** taps into extraverts' motivation. Gathering data and making learning products that will benefit others is a stronger incentive than learning something just to keep in one's mental storehouse for future possible use.

- **Projects that involve talking** energize extraverts in their learning. Projects such as interviewing, oral histories, conducting surveys, contacting resource people, performing, displaying, orally explaining, and demonstrating are examples.

For *introverted* students:

- **Working in private ways**, with internal dialogue, is more important to introverts' learning than is public dialogue. Students who prefer introverting do their best work when engrossed in mental processing. They see their mental work as private.

- **Keeping privacy when showing their work** is the introverts' preference. Introverts should always have the choice of what work products to expose and what to keep private. They usually see value in going over their work with a study partner before it is the finished product that the teacher and class see.

- **Taking enough time** to work out one's thoughts is important for everyone. Because introverting means pausing to reflect before speaking or acting, introverts want and need more time to edit and polish thoughts before putting them on public display. While extraverts enjoy editing their ideas as they talk them out, introverts want to edit privately.

- **Getting advance notice of extraverting requirements** is important for introverts so that they can prepare and don't have to ad lib. They need enough notice to allow time to prepare.

- **Reflection time that isn't interrupted** gives introverts the quiet they need for their best learning. They want teachers to schedule class time for quiet mental processing when their thoughts won't be broken into.

- **Listening and observing without pressure to turn outward** is valued by introverts. They want to know when they will be called on, and about what. They want to have certain times when they know they won't be called on, when they can just listen and observe. Much of their quality time during discussions is when they can just listen quietly and carry on an internal dialogue about what is being discussed. Research shows that the quality of students' learning in classroom dialogue has nothing to do with how often they speak or whether they speak at all.

S and N Differences in Learning: What Works

For *sensing* students:

- **Having hands-on materials** is what sensing students want at the start of a learning sequence. The sensing mental process starts best with solid, *familiar* facts and moves sequentially toward the abstractions and patterns that tie the facts together. What works best is sensory-rich experiences that engage as many of the senses as possible.

- **Going carefully and thoroughly through new material,** not skipping anything, is the sensing way of learning. Sensing students want to *know for sure* that the conclusions they reach and their work products are sound, with no gaps, and are based on facts.

- **Starting from awareness of what facts and skills the adult world values** is what sensing students want. They believe the teacher should know what skills and knowledge they will need after finishing school and college, and they expect the teacher to teach them directly. They see discovery learning as inefficient.

- **Knowing exactly what is expected of them** before they start to work gives sensing students their best start in learning something. They want a clear, detailed assignment. They value following procedures already familiar to them.

- **Using immediately the skills they learn,** not just in school-bound situations, but in their present lives outside of school, is the sensing way for best learning. It is the clear, practical usefulness of new skills and facts that convinces sensing students the new material is worth learning.

- **Using their memory for details** helps sensing students learn. They prefer to learn by using their knack for careful observation of concrete details, memorizing, and keeping a large amount of data in memory.

For *intuitive* students:

- **Beginning with the big picture** gives intuitive students a sense of going somewhere. It helps them answer the question, "Why learn this?" They want to start from the broad concepts that underlie what is to be learned before they go through hands-on materials into the details of things. They want to know where new knowledge fits into the big picture of what they already know. They resist step by step instruction that doesn't start with the global concept first.

- **Letting intuition carry them into new material** is the way intuitive students want to start. They want to move quickly to follow wherever intuition leads and let insight tell them what is meaningful and worth working on. The path of intuition is not straight or step by step.

- **Starting with something novel and fresh** catches intuitive students' imagination and sparks their learning. They look for new things to bring inspiration and the expectation of discovering something. They like beginning new things more than continuing familiar things, but when their inspiration is sustained, it carries them through to finishing what they start.

- **Choosing and directing their own work** motivates intuitive students. They like real choices in how they work out their assignments. They also like self-instruction, and finding their own intuitive way. They value opportunities to do original, inventive work.

- **Tackling new skills** is more energizing to intuitive students than practicing and honing existing ones. It is the possibilities, not the practicality, of new skills and ideas that motivate them.

- **Using their skill with language** is the way intuitives prefer to explore new things to learn. Because words are abstractions, and abstractions are at the heart of intuitive mental processing, intuitive students prefer ways to learn that give a central place to written and/or spoken language. They prefer learning *about* things and people through language, because language can give them an intuitive understanding of things quickly. They often feel slowed down in the sensing way of experiencing things and people concretely.

A Note to Teachers About Sensing and Intuition

I have made a special note here because sensing and intuition play such a key role in learning and need additional explanation. *Sensing and intuition have more to do with learning style* than the other three sets of type preferences. They are the way we pay attention to experiences and perceive the *what* that is to be learned.

The model of schooling we have all inherited puts textbooks at the center of instruction. The reading of texts and other books is primarily an intuitive activity. Reading is a process of identifying written symbols printed on the page and then attaching to the symbols meanings that relate to one's prior experiences. Symbols are abstractions, the stuff of intuitive processing. They are not concrete material. Reading about the structure of a leaf is not the same as examining a leaf to identify its structure. With reading as the primary means of learning, sensing students are put at a disadvantage. They have to make extensive use of their less-preferred mental process, intuition, which takes them more time and concentration (remember the right hand/left hand analogy). In contrast, learning outside the classroom—such as on the job training—often is an advantage to sensing learners, particularly when they can use more than one of their senses. Reading, of course, shuts out all the senses except sight.

Generally, sensing students—about two-thirds of our student population—much prefer to start learning new facts and concepts with concrete experiences, and materials other than books in their hands; then the words that follow make more sense. It is typical of intuitive students to prefer to start with the words about the new concepts, and then see examples of them. This is a contrast of major importance to education. If teachers knew nothing more than this about the types of mental processing, and if they taught so as to honor this difference between sensing and intuitive processing, I believe academic achievement data would take a dramatic jump.

How then can teachers conduct their classrooms to serve the learning needs of both sensing and intuitive students? **What works for both—at the same time?** Here are some guidelines.

- Introduce abstractions or symbols in the context of familiar facts, skills or concepts, going from the familiar to the new

- Provide sensory-rich materials *and* a big-picture context or explanation when starting a new unit or lesson

- Use textbooks as *support* for lessons, not as the center of lessons; put first-hand experience at the center of the lesson. For example, "You can start by reading what the text says about carburetors or you can start by working over here examining a carburetor and its components."

- When introducing new topics, try to tap into student interests so that their enthusiasm will help their work

- Try to have immediate practical uses for new skills you are teaching; leave a window open for intuitive students to imagine possibilities for the skills

- Teach students *how* to do projects, giving them choices in how they do them—with one choice being to do the project just as you specify in detail

T and F Differences in Learning: What Works

For students preferring *thinking*:

- **Logically constructed subject matter** and materials, and lesson activities that respond to logic, are important for T students. They are looking for cause and effect relationships among things. They value bringing logical order out of confused situations.

- **Classrooms organized in logical systems** help T students do better work. Their work suffers when they believe arbitrary, illogical order or requirements have been put on them.

- **Interesting problems to analyze** stimulate T students in their studying. They like to analyze anything of interest, to critique things and find flaws that can be fixed.
- **Classrooms free from emotional distractions** help T students concentrate on their work. Their best work comes when they feel positive without having to deal with emotional issues.

For students preferring *feeling*:

- **Subject matter to care deeply about** taps into the motivation of F students. They are looking for the human angle—the study of people to identify with and emulate, the life of the scientist or historical figure as well as the scientific principle or historical fact, and the human issue to understand and do something about.
- **Appreciation** for who they are and not just for the quality of their work is a very strong incentive for F students to do well.
- **A warm and friendly classroom,** where the teacher stays in tune with the emotional side of classroom life and deals with personal relationship issues, is where F students do their best learning.
- **Having purposes for learning based on interpersonal values,** beyond self-improvement or impersonal reasons, is what F students want to have in their studies. They want their work products to have the goal or side effect of helping others, adults and peers. A strong motivation for F students is knowing that other people depend on them, that they are important to others.

J and P Differences in Learning: What Works

For students who run their outer lives with a *judgment* process:

- **Having life organized into a clear plan** gives J students their most constructive energy. They want to know what will happen, when it will happen, and how. They look for a system that can be counted on to be consistent and predictable. J students like to have their lives organized into distinct categories, including their studies, and they like the categories to be stable. They want to have a plan for work and a plan for play, a plan for being planned and a plan for being spontaneous.
- **Teachers who are organized** are the ones J students respect most. The FJ students most want a teacher who organizes through harmonious relationships, while the TJ students are looking for logical organization in a teacher, but both types would much prefer to have whatever kind of organization is available than to cope with a teacher they see as not being predictable and scheduled.
- **Having a detailed schedule that follows priorities** helps J students do their best learning. They want to do first things first, and do check-offs as they get things done. They may become drained by changes in the schedule or priorities. Doing things out of order can be distracting to them.

- **Knowing exactly what is expected** of them, not generally but exactly, is what most J students want. This is more true for SJ students than NJs. They see the teacher as being responsible for knowing and showing them just what the world expects, just what skills are needed to function in high school, college and beyond. They would rather not have to discover these things as they go along. J students also want to know exactly what criteria and standards will be used to evaluate their work. Many of them will work at learning through a sense of duty but that is a poor substitute for clear expectations given in advance.

- **Having learning be enjoyable serious work** is a goal most J students share. J students tend to be respectful of assignments they believe are serious business, and suspicious of learning activities that seem not to be serious. Knowing the point of the activity is important. When learning activities are fun, it is important that they see the seriousness of the fun. For J students, work is work and play is play; they are separate categories. Enjoyable work is valued, but learning activities that appear to be just play are not.

- **Celebrating completions** is important to J students because they strongly value getting things finished. Ceremonies (even very small ones), certificates, or rewards (including self-rewards) to mark completions signal the value of the work done. Persistence is a trait that Js respect, and rewards that honor persistence are especially appreciated.

For students who run their outer lives with a *perception* process:

- **Following their curiosity** is what P students would like to do all the time as the main way of learning. Always open to new and interesting experiences, P students want to explore them in class as well as out. They will do their best work for the teacher who sets up lessons so they can explore the interests they have that fit within the instructional objectives. Discovering something new to them is especially energizing to P students. The organization, structure, schedules, and prescriptions that energize J students drain the P students unless the teacher organizes so as to allow them to follow their curiosity.

- **Having genuine choices in how they pursue lesson objectives** gives P students enthusiasm for learning. P students enjoy learning new things, but lose their energy for learning when the assignments of skill practice take on the feel of prescribed routine sameness, but they will work at polishing their skills when pursuing some target they themselves have chosen. When the teacher lets them find novel ways to do routine assignments, their interest is sparked and often sustained.

- **Having the stimulation of new and different experiences** is especially important to P students. Unlike the J students who are energized by predictability and continuity, P students are always alert to new stimulation for their senses or intuition. Variety in activities is their food for thought. Newness sparks their curiosity, and if the new material feeds into their ongoing interests, it can help them learn persistence and follow-through. In effect, newness and freshness of experience is essential for P students to develop sustained, deep interests.

- **Working in an ebb-and-flow style** energizes P students. In P students, the energy for learning comes in bursts, surges, and impulses, sometimes with slack periods in between. Interest in one project or task often gives way to interest in another, and a shifting of attention back and forth is common in P types. They feel little need to close one thing before switching to another. The surges are spontaneous, not directed by a plan. This ebb and flow and shifting is no more a character flaw or a sign of immaturity than is the need of J students for closure and knowing exactly what is expected of them. However, in formal education (and in many job situations) it has been regarded as a fault needing to be fixed. That view is wrong. Both J and P students should be helped to develop their skills of perception and judgment—but within their own systems of mental processing. Teachers need to recognize and accept the P students' mode of work and make plans that accommodate it within the J structure of instruction.

- **Using adaptability to solve problems** is the natural way of P students. It is natural and automatic for P students to look for emerging problems and to try to solve them with emerging solutions. This is in contrast to the J preference for planned work and predictability. In the work world, Ps are likely to be at their best in occupations that call for adaptability and ingenuity. It is in fluid learning situations rather than preset ones that P students are most energized to learn. When they have confidence in handling such tasks as part of their academic work, they will then have energy available to channel into developing the J skills of persistence and planning.

- **Having work that feels like play** is when P students do their best. Generally, they do not have distinct categories of work and play, as do the J students. For J students, play is a reward for work completed. P students want to make their work as playful as possible to bring energy and interest into it. For them, interesting work feels like play. The teacher who isn't sure how to help P students make their work playful can ask them and they will generally have good suggestions.

A Note to Teachers About Judgment and Perception

Next to the importance of using S and N differences in planning effective instruction is using an understanding of J and P differences in helping students study effectively. Educational institutions operate by the clock, by settled rules and procedures, by planned curriculums and lessons, by people in organized relationships. It is a J world where judgments already have been made, systems are in place, and things are running according to the systems and schedules. People who run their outer lives with a judgment mental process (thinking judgment or feeling judgment), in general, value this kind of structured life in schools. They make up a little more than half of the population.

It is not surprising that two-thirds of the people attracted to the teaching profession are Js. With J teachers and J administrators being in the majority and operating the schools, it is also no surprise that P students often express the feeling that school and college don't encourage their best work. When teachers and administrators do not know about the mental processing types and the JP contrast, they tend to see the P students' spontaneous behavior as immaturity. They see the P behavior as impulsiveness that mature people have learned to control, as inappropriate behavior to be trained out of them. This is not a constructive point of view—J behavior being seen as a model for all to follow, and P behavior being treated as a deficit. The path to maturity in all the types is within their own mental framework. In this case, the path for young Ps to emulate is a mature P path, just as the path for young Js is a J mature model.

The J model is a familiar one. All the books and other resources concerned with teaching study skills and self-management (the ones I am aware of) draw upon the J model and try to teach all students to follow the J way. The P pathway is much less familiar. I described the basics of it in the previous section. Here are some tips for running the classroom so as to give a legitimate place for the P way of learning.

Students' preference for the J or P way of running their outer lives will generally be quite visible to the teacher. The more immature students will be the more obvious as to their preference. The immature J will want to know *exactly* what the teacher expects; be unsettled by any change in expectations; be quick to put a plan in place, even when it is poorly thought out; get at it quickly to get it finished and out of the way; and resist or resent any subsequent change in the plan suggested by the teacher. The immature P may take a long time getting started on assignments, seeming to be easily distracted by whatever else might be interesting; change direction in a project at any point as he or she thinks of something better; not be aware of the time it takes to get things done; procrastinate against a deadline; and finish in a rush as the deadline closes in, or miss the deadline and ask for an extension. Mature P students will have begun to figure out ways to cope with the J system, and mature J students have begun to find out how to avoid the pitfalls that go with a J preference.

Here are some techniques that teachers have used successfully to **accommodate both J and P ways** of working on learning tasks.

- Plan ahead, and make the plan visible to students, so that J students can see a predictable structure. The J students will work better if they have each week's agenda by the Friday before. It won't bother the P students. A long-term agenda helps too.

- Demonstrate organization. Make visible to students your own mental work of organizing, at times explaining how you arrived at decisions. Many students need this kind of living model of the planning process.

- Build exploring time into your plans. Include labs and projects that spark curiosity and let students investigate in their own ways. P students thrive on it, and J students will be engaged if they understand it is serious work and part of a plan.

- Write individual contracts with students, giving them real choices in how they do and report their work. In this kind of contract system, students remain accountable for outcomes, and perhaps some processes of studying, but are free to decide, with teacher approval, how to reach the outcomes. Some J students will want one of the contract choices to be a prescription of exactly what to do and how to do it.

- Fold student interests into lesson plans and assignments. Pursuing and protecting their interests helps J students exercise their perception processes, and helps P students exercise their judgment processes.

- Do not penalize P students for their ebb and flow style of working, but hold them accountable for products and deadlines.

- Help students learn how to do backwards planning; that is, begin at the deadline and move back toward the present to see what steps in one's work have to be done by when and what other time commitments have to be taken into account in the plan to meet the deadline. This is especially important for P students who will be less realistic about the time it takes to get things done.

- Make clear up front your system of accountability—objectives, expectations, requirements, deadlines and evaluative criteria—and give the students plenty of advance notice.

- Consider giving students intermediate deadlines. Some students, mostly Ps, will want to keep gathering data without closing down to a definite plan, and will be unrealistic about time as they move toward the final deadline. They will benefit from having progress report deadlines when they have to show you completed segments of their work.

- Plan for student projects and other assignments that promote adaptability and ingenuity.

  P students thrive on them and J students need them so as to stretch themselves.

- Be sure that students understand that the fun work you plan is serious learning. J students need to be reassured that it isn't just play. P students won't care whether the fun is serious. Allow students to do and report their work in playful ways. That will be important to Ps.

How the Preferences Affect Learning

The tables on the next four pages show the learning preferences in a different way. The material you have just read is summarized and presented in the tables in column form so that the contrasts between the preference pairs are easier to see.

HOW THE E AND I PREFERENCES AFFECT LEARNING

EXTRAVERSION

Cognitive style: The extraversion preference is expressed as a cognitive style that favors:
- learning by talking and physically engaging the environment,
- letting attention flow outward toward objective events,
- talking to help thoughts to form and become clear,
- learning through interactions, verbal and non-verbal.

Study style: Extraverted study styles favor:
- acting first, reflecting after,
- plunging into new material,
- starting interactions needed to stimulate reflection and concentration,
- having a strong, interesting, external reason for studying, beyond learning for its own sake,
- avoiding distractions that will cut into their concentration,
- studying with a friend,
- studying to prepare to teach someone.

Instruction that fits Es: The extraverting types do their best work with:
- opportunities to think out loud; e.g., one-to- one with the teacher, classroom discussions, working with another student, action projects involving people,
- learning activities that have an effect outside the learner, such as visible results from a project,
- teachers who manage classroom dialogue so that extraverts have ways to clarify their ideas aloud before they add them to class discussion,
- assignments that let them see what other people are doing and what they regard as important.

INTROVERSION

Cognitive style: The introversion preference is expressed as a cognitive style that favors:
- quiet reflection,
- keeping one's thoughts inside until they are polished,
- letting attention flow inward,
- being engrossed in inner events: ideas, impressions, concepts,
- learning in private, individual ways.

Study style: Introverted study styles favor:
- reflecting first, acting after (if necessary),
- looking for new data to fit into the internal dialogue that is always going on,
- working privately—perhaps checking one's work with someone who is trusted,
- reading as the main way of studying,
- listening to others talk about the topic being studied, and privately processing what they take in,
- extraverting just when they choose to.

Instruction that fits Is: The introverting types like learning situations that let them:
- work internally with their own thoughts: listening, observing, lab work, reading, writing,
- process experiences at their own pace,
- present the results of their work in forms that let them keep their privacy,
- have ample time to polish their work inside before needing to present it,
- have time to reflect before answering the teacher's questions.
- tie their studies to their own personal interests, their internal agenda.

From *People Types and Tiger Stripes*, 3rd edition, Gordon Lawrence, 1993.

HOW THE S AND N PREFERENCES AFFECT LEARNING

SENSING

Cognitive style: The sensing preference is expressed in a cognitive style that favors:
- being careful to get the facts right,
- memory of facts,
- observing specifics, absorbing data,
- starting with concrete experience, then moving to the abstract,
- aiming toward soundness of understanding,
- staying connected to practical realities around oneself,
- attending to what is in the present moment.

Study style: The sensing preference is associated with a study style that favors:
- a practical approach to new material, looking for immediate usefulness,
- beginning with the familiar, solid facts of their own personal experience, and distilling abstractions and principles from them.

Instruction that fits Ss: Sensing types do their best work with:
- instruction that allows them to hear and touch as well as see (or only read about) what they are learning
- hands-on labs, materials that can be handled,
- relevant films and other audio-visuals,
- computer-assisted instruction,
- first-hand experience that gives practice in the skills and concepts to be learned,
- teachers who provide concrete experiences first in any learning sequence, before using the textbook,
- teachers who show them exactly what facts and skills the adult world expects of them,
- teachers who do not move "too quickly" through material, touching just the high spots or jumping from thought to thought,
- assignments that allow them to start with known facts before having to imagine possibilities,
- skills and facts they can use in their present lives.

INTUITION

Cognitive style: The intuition preference is expressed in a cognitive style that prefers:
- being caught up in inspiration,
- moving quickly in seeing meanings and associations,
- reading between the lines,
- relying on insight more than careful observation,
- relying on easy use of words more than on memory of facts,
- focusing on general concepts more than details and practical facts.

Study style: Intuitives typically adopt a study style that includes:
- following inspirations,
- jumping in to new material,
- finding their own way through new material,
- wanting the big picture first, before details,
- exploring new skills rather than polishing present ones.

Instruction that fits Ns: The intuitive types do their best work with:
- assignments that put them on their own initiative,
- real choices in the ways they work out their assignments,
- opportunities to be inventive and original,
- opportunities for self-instruction, individually or with a group,
- a system of individual contracts between teacher and students,
- fascinating new possibilities,
- experiences rich with complexities,
- work that stays fresh by calling for new skills, not just repetition of existing skills,
- teachers with a brisk pace, who don't go "too slowly"

From *People Types and Tiger Stripes*, 3rd edition, Gordon Lawrence, 1993.

LOOKING AT TYPE AND LEARNING STYLES

HOW THE T AND F PREFERENCES AFFECT LEARNING

THINKING

Cognitive style: A preference for thinking judgment is expressed in a cognitive style that favors:

- making impersonal judgments,
- aiming toward objective truth,
- analyzing experiences to find logical principles underlying them,
- keeping mental life in order through logical principles,
- staying cool and free of emotional concerns while making decisions,
- naturally critiquing things, finding flaws to fix, aiming toward clarity and precision.

Study style: The thinking preference is reflected in a study style that favors:

- logically constructed subject matter,
- classrooms organized in logical systems,
- classrooms free from emotional distractions,
- interesting problems to analyze,
- wanting to bring logical order out of confused situations,
- wanting to get mastery over material.

Instruction that fits Ts: The thinking types do their best work with:

- teachers who are logically organized
- subjects that show cause and effect relationships,
- subjects that respond to logic,
- feedback that shows them specific, objective achievement.

FEELING

Cognitive style: A preference for feeling judgment is expressed in a cognitive style that favors:

- making caring judgments,
- taking into account people's motives and personal values,
- attending to the relationships between people, seeking harmony,
- personalizing issues and causes that have high priority,
- staying tuned to emotional aspects of life,
- naturally appreciating people and things.

Study style: Students who prefer feeling judgment usually favor:

- having topics to study that they care deeply about, with a human angle to them,
- learning through personal relationships rather than impersonal, individualized activities,
- warm and friendly classrooms,
- learning by helping, responding to other's needs.

Instruction that fits Fs: The feeling types do their best work with:

- teachers who value personal rapport with students,
- assignments that have a goal of contributing to others,
- receiving appreciation for them as persons,
- harmonious small-group work.

From *People Types and Tiger Stripes*, 3rd edition, Gordon Lawrence, 1993.

HOW THE J AND P PREFERENCES AFFECT LEARNING

JUDGMENT

Cognitive style: Running one's outer life with a judgment process is expressed as a cognitive style that favors:
- having a clear structure in a learning situation from the beginning,
- aiming toward completions and getting closure,
- having life organized into an orderly plan,
- looking for consistency, wanting to be able to predict how things will come out..

Study style: J types typically adopt a study style that includes:
- planful and scheduled work, drawing energy from the steady, orderly process of doing their work,
- wanting to know exactly what they are accountable for and by what standards they will be judged,
- seeing assignments as serious business, and persisting in doing them.

Instruction that fits Js: The J types do their best work with:
- preplanned structure, and a teacher who carefully provides it,
- predictability and consistency,
- formalized instruction that moves in orderly sequences,
- prescribed tasks,
- milestones, completion points, ceremonies to honor successful completions.

PERCEPTION

Cognitive style: Running one's outer life with a perception process is expressed as a cognitive style that favors:
- open exploration without a preplanned structure,
- staying open to new experiences,
- managing emerging problems with plans that emerge with the problems,
- having the stimulation of something new and different.

Study style: P types typically adopt a study style that includes:
- spontaneously following their curiosity,
- studying when the surges of impulsive energy come to them,
- studying to discover something new to them,
- finding novel ways to do routine assignments so as to spark enough interest to do the assignments.

Instruction that fits Ps: The P types do their best work when:
- they can pursue problems in their own way,
- they have genuine choices in assignments, as with a system of individual contracts in which the student can negotiate some of the activities,
- assignments hold their interest,
- their work feels like play.

From *People Types and Tiger Stripes*, 3rd edition, Gordon Lawrence, 1993.

LOOKING AT TYPE AND LEARNING STYLES

Questions Often Asked About Type And Learning Style

As you think about the differences in learning styles, what questions come to mind? Here are some questions that often are asked when I work with a group of students or teachers.

Aren't some of the learning styles better than others for doing well in school (or college)?

Students who do well come in all types. There is nothing about a type preference that limits you in learning well. Different learning situations call for different preferences. For example, in some situations, such as ad lib presentations, the extraversion preference has an advantage, and in other situations, such as extended quiet concentration, the preference for introversion works better. What's needed is to develop the skills that different situations require: an extravert needs introverting skills, but needs to develop them *in an extravert's way*—and vice versa for introverts. In the section that follows are some tips for building skills that come less naturally to us because of our type preferences.

The J and P preferences tell us a lot about study style, and in many school and college learning situations the J preference has an advantage. The J preference is not better, but it represents a study style that fits more easily into the academic world of learning by the calendar and clock. The J way of studying gets energy from having a plan and schedule, and making steady progress toward completions. That fits the way most teachers give assignments, set deadlines, and award grades.

The P way of studying, drawing energy from surges of interest, is a different way, but not better or worse. The research on type and learning does not show that Js learn more than Ps. But the research does suggest that the natural J drive toward closure gives Js an advantage in fitting their learning into the system that awards grades. Time management and a system for meeting deadlines are skills that all students have to learn, but P students have to work harder at these skills because they are not part of the natural rhythm of their learning process. Some ideas to help Ps develop these skills may be found in the next section..

Are type and learning style really the same thing?

No. One's type of mental processing is a factor in one's learning style, but some learning strategies are independent of type. Some habits of learning come from type. They might be called instinctive ways of learning. All of us have techniques of learning that were taught to us or we taught ourselves. Similarly, there are motivations and values that are linked to type, and others that are independent of type.

If learning style and type are different, what's gained by learning about type?

Learning about the type preferences helps us harness the natural type-based motivations for learning that will give us better results from our studying. We can shape our own learning styles to a large extent, but we don't change to another type of mental processing. The aspects of our learning styles that reflect our types can be expected to persist across situations. We can count on our understanding of type to help us use our mental resources better—however the learning situations may change.

If my type stays the same across situations, am I stuck with the learning style I now have?

No. Improving our learning strategies and habits is something we all can do, continuously. As we learn the new strategies, of course, our type of mental processing remains the same—and it gives us the means to make the changes. As we try out new learning techniques, the ones that will work best and stick with us are ones that fit the kind of mental energy and values that go with our type.

So, I improve within my type but don't change my type?

Yes. Your type is a framework within which your development happens. If your best-fit type is ENFP, for example, you want to aim for the assets of well-developed ENFP. That is a life-long process. You also will need to develop some skills that are more associated with I, S, T, and J. These skills will supplement your ENFP nature, but will always be in service to it, and not change you to another type. As you grow within your type, you will also improve your learning strategies as part of the process. Your best satisfactions in life will come through the assets of your type.

Tips For Using Type

Adjusting to a teacher. Considering that there are 16 types, the chances are good that most teachers you encounter have types different from yours. The variety and fresh viewpoints you get from them may be an advantage, if you experience the type differences constructively. If you have a particular teacher who is difficult for you to tune in to, a type contrast may be the reason. How can you bridge the difference? Read the preceding pages that show the EI, SN, TF, and JP contrasts. Think of the description opposite yours as a style to which the teacher might prefer to teach. Research shows that teachers do prefer to teach in a way that satisfies their own way of learning. For example, if you are an S, and believe the teacher may be an N, or vice versa, you can test your hypothesis this way to see how the teacher's mental processing goes.

Next look at your learning style description, in the last section of the book. Does the description show you some things to ask the teacher that will help you learn better? Teachers wants you to do your best learning, but they may not know what instructional tools will help you do your best work. You will have to come up with requests to make of the teacher—reasonable requests—for options and assistance that will help you study better. For example, if you are an S with an N teacher whose lectures are hard for you to follow, the SN pages above will give you some clues as to why, and ideas for what to do about the situation. In this case, you might try asking for examples or specific applications of the general concepts the teacher is providing.

Study style. The most important advice I can give you is to work from the strengths of your type. That advice certainly applies to studying. Extraverts should find a **study partner** to talk with, and remove distractions when you have to study alone. For introverted students, studying alone makes sense, but do a trial run with a partner when you have to make an oral presentation. **Outlining** of important things to remember is valuable for both S and N students, but for different reasons. It helps Ss find the main points, the big picture within the details. It helps Ns to attend to details and organize them around the main points. **Skimming** text material is easy for most Ns, but it is a skill that Ss have to develop so they can see the patterns and key ideas in the writing. Finding and pumping up your own **motivation for studying** is important. Reread the section on motivation. For example, the motivation of F types to study impersonal material depends, at least in part, on finding ways to personalize it, to link it to personal values.

Time management is a major issue for Ps. Most schools and colleges have opportunities to learn about time management techniques. As a P myself, I have found that **backwards planning** helps me. That is, I start planning a project by working backwards from the deadline, thinking about all the things that will compete for time against this project, between now and the deadline. Then I divide the project into components, and estimate the minutes or hours it will take to complete each. As an N, I know that my time estimations are usually too optimistic, so I usually double my estimate. I also set for myself (and my students) **intermediate deadlines** as a way of seeing whether the components are getting done on time. That way the crunch of the deadline helps me all along and not just at the end.

Js have a different kind of time management problem. Wanting to envision the finished product from the beginning of the project, they often decide too quickly what it will look like at the end and shut down too soon the search for data they need to construct a good quality product. Their time management problem is resistance to flexing the schedule to allow openings for new data and changes in the scheduled steps. Building **quality check** steps into the schedule helps them. That is, steps for getting someone else to look at their progress and make suggestions for improvements.

Preparing for tests. Some interesting research on type and test taking has been done on several college campuses. The research shows that students who learn about their type and use that knowledge can improve their grades on tests. Of course, I expected those results. The part of the research that especially interested me was the findings about SN differences in how students have problems in taking tests. When taking multiple-choice tests with time limits on them, sensing students and intuitive students had very different kinds of problems.

The Ss got into trouble by reading each item so thoroughly before answering that their pace wasn't fast enough to finish all the items. By following a simple piece of advice they were able to significantly raise scores next time around. The advice was: Force yourself to answer the item after reading it only once, carefully. When you get to the end of the test you can revisit any items you want to look at again. Why did this advice work to raise scores? Sensing types tend to distrust their intuition, which would have to be used if they answered after just one reading of an item. They weren't aware that their intuition was working for them all the time, and they could trust it to give them a good hunch—even when they felt they hadn't taken enough time to get all the S cues of the test questions. If they had done their homework, they could trust their intuition.

The intuitive students who had done their homework but still scored less well on timed tests than had been expected had a different kind of trouble. They read too much into the questions. Their intuition kept trying to scope out "what the test writer was really trying to get at," and expected to find some trick or shade of meaning they should take into account. This mental habit was causing them to pick the wrong response sometimes. The piece of advice that worked for them was: Take the most literal, obvious possible meaning of the question and answer it that way. Most test writers intend to have only straight-forward questions with no tricks. These two sets of advice apply as well to multiple-choice tests that have no time limits.

When taking essay tests, the advice is to watch out for your blind spots. Sensing types tend to do well in reporting facts they have learned, but may be weak on giving a clear introduction, linking their facts together into the big picture of the essay, and giving a good conclusion or summary. Intuitive types have the opposite problems in their essay responses: good openings and endings, and good ideas, but weak on supporting facts, and sometimes getting caught up in taking such a creative angle that they miss the main intention of the test question.

Next steps. See the Further Resources section for other books about using type to help you do your best learning. I hope you will find this book worth rereading as you continue to use the ideas of type. CAPT, the publisher of this book, has many other resources about type you can use in other areas of your life.

The Sixteen Learning Styles

ENTJ learning style

For ENTJs, the best learning happens when they are in charge of managing themselves and others in pursuing a task that challenges their intuition. Being in charge gives them extra energy and purpose for learning something new. They want to master the skills they need, to have opportunities to actively practice them, and to show their competence.

Logical order and action. ENTJs highly value and work best in environments that are logically and efficiently structured, and they want teachers to maintain that kind of classroom. They also thrive on action and want opportunities to learn things in active ways, including talking. Especially as children, sitting still and listening is not a comfortable or efficient way for them to learn.

Talk to learn. ENTJs like learning situations that give them a chance to talk; for example, one-to-one with the teacher, classroom discussions, action projects involving people, and making oral presentations. They value these opportunities to "think out loud." They often say they do their best thinking when they are talking —their thoughts become clear as they speak them. Writing helps them too.

Mental work. ENTJs want their lives systematically organized by principles they have adopted through logical analysis. They appreciate the kind of instruction that gives them the time and opportunity for this mental work. ENTJs describe their minds as a continuous flow of ideas and possibilities. They construct and reconstruct mental models of their ideas, envisioning how things could be made or done. Teachers will be most effective with them when they call attention to the context, principles, conceptual organizers, and/or broad meanings of things first—before beginning to focus on facts, skills, and specifics.

New ideas. They like to explore new ideas. Their kind of mind is quick in seeing associations and meanings, reading between the lines, and grasping general concepts. Concentrating on general meanings, they often overlook details and practical matters. They rely on insight more than on careful observation, and on their skill with words more than on memory of facts. They say their minds work best when they feel objective and free from emotional concerns, and they like learning situations that let them work that way.

Inquiry learning. ENTJs are naturally curious about almost anything that engages their curiosity. As children, they want to do a great variety of things, their curiosity often taking them into exploring things and places the teacher or parent did not have in mind for them. They like learning assignments that put them on their own initiative and give them opportunities for self-instruction. They like to find their own way through new material and invent their own ways to solve problems. They also like an organized lecture if they believe the teacher is competent. Whether by lecture or other means, they prefer instruction to be planned and formalized, and to flow in a logical and orderly way. They see reading and writing as valuable *if* they are using them to pursue something important to themselves.

Planning. ENTJs want their goals and schedules planned at the beginning. Having a plan in mind helps them feel free to concentrate on the problems to be solved. They draw energy from the steady, orderly process of working, taking pleasure from each completion as they move toward the end of the job. They like milestones to acknowledge completions. If their drive toward closure blocks out ideas and data they should give attention to, the effective teacher helps them see the usefulness of holding off closure until they have examined other possibilities that may be important to their plans.

ESTJ learning style

For ESTJs, the best learning happens when they are in charge of managing a practical, clear-cut task for which they know they are responsible and accountable. Being in charge and organizing other people gives them extra energy and purpose for learning something new. When the purpose is clear and important, they see their school learning as serious work. They believe the adult world has specific skills and facts they should master, and they want the teacher to focus instruction on those concrete realities. They want to be shown clearly what is expected of them and do not want to waste time discovering it for themselves.

Logical order and action. Because ESTJs highly value order and work best in environments that are logically and efficiently organized, they may resent and resist a teacher who does not maintain that kind of classroom. They also thrive on action and want opportunities to learn things in physically active ways, including talking as a means of processing their thoughts. Especially as children, sitting still and listening is not a comfortable or efficient way for them to learn. ESTJs want their lives ordered by principles they have adopted through logical analysis and first-hand experience. They say their minds work best when they feel objective and free from emotional concerns. They want learning situations that let them work in these ways.

Clear purposes. For ESTJs to learn best, they first want to have a clear statement of what the instruction is about; then to see (and hear and touch, if possible) an example and demonstration of what is to be learned; then have practice, with assistance available, until no more help is needed. Often they are helped by relevant, good quality audio-visual presentations, labs, materials that can be handled, and computer-assisted instruction, but first-hand, concrete experience is best.

Goal oriented. ESTJs want their goals clearly in mind as they work. Goals and schedules planned at the beginning help them feel free to concentrate on the specifics of the task. They draw energy from the steady, orderly process of working, taking pleasure from each small completion as they move toward the end of the job. They like milestones to acknowledge completions. Sometimes their drive toward closure blocks out ideas and data they should give attention to. The effective teacher helps them see the usefulness of holding off closure until they have examined other facts that may be important to their plans.

Reading may not be their first choice of ways to learn about new things. ESTJ children can and do enjoy reading if they are taught it correctly, step by step, as a code that is interesting to break. If not taught correctly, extraverts with a preference for sensing, such as ESTJs, may neglect or resist reading because it engages only the sense of sight and is usually done alone, quietly. But when they are confident in their ability to read, they appreciate the efficiency it brings as a learning tool. They want their reading materials to be clear, lively, action-oriented, and based on proven experience.

Sound and practical. ESTJs thrive on learning tasks that use their ability to observe specifics and organize them. They rely a lot on their knack for memorizing. But things that are memorized are likely to be lost unless they become meaningful through practical use. When studying subjects they care about, they go carefully and thoroughly through the material, wanting to have their understanding be sound and accurate. They want to have their facts straight and logically organized.

Here-and-now usefulness. ESTJs like to acquire knowledge step by step. They get frustrated with the teacher who moves too quickly through material, touching just abstract ideas or jumping from thought to thought. They do their best work when their assignments clearly connect with the practical realities of their present lives, and they can best learn principles and theories by extracting them from their own concrete actions. They believe in studying for the future, such as studying specifically for a career, but not just because "someday you'll need it." While they will learn something out of a sense of duty and responsibility, they learn best when tackling something useful for their present interests.

From concrete to abstract. ESTJs prefer instruction to be formalized and to flow in a logical and orderly way, from concrete to abstract. Most textbooks, especially beyond the elementary school, present abstractions first, followed (sometimes) by concrete examples. This sequence runs against the thought processes of ESTJs. Their teacher can provide a bridge by arranging concrete learning experiences first in any learning sequence, before using the textbook.

INTP learning style

For INTPs, the best learning comes when they are quietly absorbed in analyzing problems that interest them. They like working on tough, abstract problems—especially when other people have given up on them. INTPs can easily be bored with assignments that seem routine to them. They are naturally curious about almost anything that engages their imagination, but they reserve most of their attention for a few special interests that they pursue in their own individual, private way—often far afield from the assignment the teacher has made. Highly independent, they often prefer to teach themselves whatever they believe they need to know, when they need to know it. This preference may explain why INTPs are often found making extensive use of computers. However, while they favor teaching themselves, they are also willing to have a competent teacher make a contribution too.

Mental priorities. INTPs describe their minds as a continuous flow of ideas and possibilities. They construct and reconstruct mental models of their ideas, envisioning how things could be made or done. Their kind of mind is quick in seeing associations and meanings, reading between the lines, and grasping general concepts. Concentrating on general meanings, they often overlook details and practical matters, sometimes neglecting to test their ideas for practical soundness. They rely on insight more than on careful observation, and on conceptual skills more than on their memory of facts.

Logical thinking. They take a detached, analytical approach to life. Logic is paramount for INTPs, and they feel a need to keep their mental life ordered by abstract principles they have adopted through logical analysis. Good instruction gives them the time and opportunity for this kind of mental work. They say their minds work best when they are free from the distractions of emotional concerns, and they like learning situations that let them work that way.

Reading. One of their main ways of learning is reading and with most INTPs being avid readers, they like learning assignments that put them on their own initiative and give them opportunities for self-instruction through reading. They also look for opportunities to be inventive and original.

Study style. The INTP study style is spontaneous, flowing with surges of impulsive energy toward whatever pulls their curiosity. Their open and exploring approach to learning does not fit easily within set plans and schedules. They find it hard to predict when the impulse to study will come. Because they want to go deeply into what interests them, they will study with great energy and concentration when their learning assignments coincide with their interests. When they can discipline themselves to focus this energy on less interesting tasks, INTPs teach themselves how to fit into institutional schedules.

They like beginnings a lot more than endings, because beginnings are fired with the fascination of new possibilities. When they have study assignments they can be enthusiastic about, they are much more likely to carry them to the finish line.

Informal problem solving. INTPs appreciate systematically organized instruction, but they want it to allow for informal problem solving, in contrast to the preplanned structure of most textbooks and teaching methods. In high school and beyond, they generally like well organized and competent lectures, but with some time saved for other kinds of learning as well. They are at their best when the instruction calls for them to manage emerging problems, as in some educational games and laboratory work. They do well with assignments that provide for low structure and inductive exploration. They also like to take a playful approach to their work, and do their best work when it feels like play. For them, learning is a private matter, so the play may be mental play that doesn't involve other people.

Invention and choice. INTPs like to invent their own ways to solve problems, and enjoy independent study. Unless they have some real choices in the ways they work out their assignments, they may resist in various ways and do only what they want. They do well with a system of individual contracts between teacher and students, in which students can negotiate some activities.

ISTP learning style

For ISTPs, the best learning happens when they are quietly absorbed in observing, analyzing, and finding the logical principles that underlie the facts they encounter. They are naturally curious about almost anything that engages their senses, but they reserve most of their attention for a few special interests that they pursue in their own individual, private way.

Sensory learning. They learn mainly through their senses, doing best with instruction that allows them to hear and touch as well as see what they are learning. Often they are helped by relevant, good quality audio-visual presentations, labs, materials that can be handled, and computer-assisted instruction. They appreciate computers and other learning resources that give them first-hand experience and allow them to work at their own pace and in their own way as they master what is important to them. They do their best work when their learning assignments clearly connect with the practical realities of their present lives. Reading, which engages only the sense of sight, is not an adequate substitute for multi-sensory learning for ISTP children. But they can master reading and enjoy it, especially if it is taught in concrete ways, as a code that is interesting to break. When they are confident in their ability to read, they appreciate the efficiency it brings as a learning tool. They want their reading material to be clear, factual, straightforward, and based on proven experience.

Logical thinking. Logic is paramount for ISTPs, and they feel a need to keep their mental life ordered by principles they have adopted through logical analysis. Good instruction gives them the time and opportunity for this kind of mental work. They say their minds work best when they feel objective and free from emotional concerns, and they like learning situations that let them work that way. They respect a teacher who is logically organized, who provides practical, objective material for them to study, and holds them accountable for what was assigned.

Concrete, reflective learning. Being inward-focused thinkers who value exact facts and logical systems, ISTPs want their instruction to flow in logical sequences, from concrete to abstract. They learn abstract principles and concepts by distilling them out of concrete experiences, especially their own direct experience. Most textbooks, especially beyond the elementary school, present abstractions first, followed (sometimes) by concrete examples. This sequence runs against the thought processes of ISTPs. Their teacher can provide a bridge by arranging concrete learning experiences first in any learning sequence, before using the textbook.

Orderly, factual learning. They thrive on tasks that require observation of specifics and memory of facts. They go through new material carefully until they find a system by which they can grasp it soundly. ISTPs disliked being rushed, and want ample time for quiet mental processing. Wanting exact data, they get frustrated with the teacher who moves too quickly through material, touching just the high spots or jumping from thought to thought, expecting them to fill in the gaps with their intuition. Being naturally observant of details in the here and now, they tend to overlook the big picture and general meanings. They prefer teachers and textbooks that help them stay in touch with the key points by using illustrations, graphs, tables, and summaries.

Study style. The ISTP study style is spontaneous, flowing with surges of impulsive energy toward whatever pulls their curiosity. Their open and exploring approach to learning does not fit easily within set plans and schedules. They find it hard to predict when the impulse to study will come. Because they want to go deeply into what interests them, they will study with great intensity, energy, and concentration when their learning assignments coincide with their interests. Their intense study style, often pushing to get perfection, keeps them focused on one task at a time. They prefer not to handle several tasks at once.

Informal problem solving. ISTPs appreciate systematically organized instruction, but they want it to allow for informal problem solving, in contrast to the preplanned structure of most textbooks and teaching methods. They are at their best when the instruction calls for them to manage emerging problems, as in laboratory work. They do well with assignments that provide for structured, hands-on exploratory observation as opposed to low structure and inductive exploration. Unless ISTPs have some real choices in the ways they work out their assignments, they may resist and not do them. They usually do well with a system of individual contracts between teacher and students, in which students can negotiate some activities. They also like to take a playful approach to their work, and they do their best work when it feels like play.

ENFJ Learning Style

For ENFJs, the best learning flows from interactions with others. They respond with high energy to the teacher who takes a personal interest in them and gives them individual feedback. Naturally concerned with harmony in relationships, they feel their energy for studying drained away by abrasiveness in the learning setting.

Active learning. As children, ENFJs especially like learning activities that allow them to learn through interactions; for example, one-to-one with the teacher, classroom discussions, study groups, studying with a friend, action projects involving people, and making oral presentations. ENFJs value these kinds of opportunities to "think out loud." They often say they do their best thinking when they are talking—their thoughts become clear as they speak them, especially to friendly listeners.

They want to talk to learn *if* the classroom is a cooperative, orderly, and friendly place where they will not have to feel on guard about what they say. Otherwise, they would rather have instruction that does not require talking. In high school and beyond, they usually like a lecture-style presentation because it lets them concentrate on the subject without their feeling personally obligated to try to maintain harmony in group-style learning activities.

Goal oriented. ENFJs want their goals clearly in mind as they work. Goals and schedules planned at the beginning help them feel free to concentrate and effectively use their creative energies. They want opportunities to be creative and original, and can do that best when the teacher lets them have choices in the ways they work toward their goals. They also draw energy from the orderly process of doing their work, taking pleasure from each small completion as they move toward the end of the job.

ENFJs usually have more interests and projects in mind that they have time to work on. They want to get closure on the project at hand so they can get on with the next one. If their drive toward closure blocks out ideas and data they should give attention to, the effective teacher helps them see the usefulness of holding off closure until they examine other data or possibilities that may be important to them, and complete their work with care.

Self-critical. With high expectations for themselves, ENFJs often are very self-critical. Because of their self-criticism, they may feel very hurt by teacher feedback that seems to heap still more criticism on them. The teacher will be more successful by taking care in finding out what the ENFJ is trying to do and then coaching with suggestions.

Favored instruction. ENFJs respond best to a teacher who is enthusiastic, even-handed and respectful of students, and maintains a harmonious learning setting. ENFJs want their instruction to be structured, with an orderly flow. They expect to be held accountable, and they want to know just what is expected of them. They need milestones, markers of completions, and they like to reward themselves for jobs done. Reading, silently or aloud, suits them and they usually enjoy reading to learn. Writing helps them too. Many ENFJs enjoy tutoring or helping other students, with the outcome often being that they themselves learn better in the helping role.

Mental processing. ENFJs describe their minds as a continuous flow of ideas—wonderings about experiences, particularly about people—with all ideas related to each other in complex ways. Their kind of mind is quick in seeing associations and meanings, reading between the lines, and grasping general concepts. Concentrating on general meanings, they run the risk of overlooking details and practical matters—especially in matters that have no bearing on the personal relationships they maintain. They rely on insight more than on sensory observation, and on verbal fluency more than on their memory of facts.

Problem solving. They prefer to solve problems by weighing value issues in the context of deeply held beliefs and personal priorities. They want to make decisions that take into account other people's needs and concerns, and they are wary of impersonal reasoning and arguments that do not attend adequately to feelings. They want to find harmonious solutions to problems, to bring people along by showing appreciation and interest in them. They tend to tackle impersonal problems by converting them into personal ones so that they can use their people skills in solving them.

ESFJ Learning Style

For ESFJs, the best learning flows from personal relationships. They respond with high energy to the teacher who takes a personal interest in them and gives them individual feedback. Being keenly concerned with harmony in relationships, they feel their energy for studying drained away by abrasiveness in the learning setting. ESFJs tend to be self-critical, and may feel very hurt by teacher feedback that seems to heap still more criticism on them. The teacher will be more successful by taking care in finding out what the ESFJ is trying to do and then coaching with concrete suggestions.

Active learning. As children, they especially like learning through interactions; for example, one- to-one with the teacher, classroom discussions, study groups, studying with a friend, activities outside the classroom involving people, student-led presentations, and tutoring a child. ESFJs value these active kinds of opportunities to "think out loud." They often say they do their best thinking when they are talking—their thoughts become clear as they speak them. They want to talk to learn *if* the classroom is a cooperative, orderly, and friendly place where they will not have to feel on guard about what they say. Otherwise, they would rather have instruction that does not require talking. In high school and beyond, they usually like a lecture-style presentation—often taking detailed notes—because it lets them concentrate on the subject without their feeling personally obligated to try to maintain harmony in group-style learning activities.

Sensory learning. ESFJs do best with instruction that allows them to hear and touch as well as see what they are learning. They want the teacher to give examples and demonstrate what is to be learned, then guide their practice until no more help is needed. They may be helped by good quality television, films, audio-visual presentations, materials that can be handled, labs, and computer-assisted instruction, but concrete, first-hand experience is best. Reading, which engages only the sense of sight, may not be their first choice of ways to learn about new things. ESFJs can and do enjoy reading if it is taught in multi-sensory and social ways. They need to be taught reading step by step, as a code that is interesting to break. When they become confident in their ability to read, they can become avid readers.

Goal oriented. ESFJs want their goals planned ahead and clearly in mind as they work. They draw energy from the steady, orderly process of working toward the end of the job, with markers to acknowledge completions. Frequent appreciation shown for the ESFJ's progress is especially helpful. Sometimes their drive toward closure blocks out ideas and data they should give attention to. The effective teacher helps them see the usefulness of holding off closure until they have examined other important facts. They want to do their studying thoroughly, always aiming for sound understanding, and they do not want to be rushed. They get frustrated with the teacher who moves too quickly through material, touching just the high spots or jumping from thought to thought. They do not want to be required to fill in the gaps with their intuition.

From concrete to abstract. ESFJs want their instruction to flow step by step, from concrete to abstract. They learn abstract principles and concepts by distilling them out of their own concrete experience. Most textbooks present abstractions first, followed (sometimes) by concrete examples. This sequence runs against the thought processes of ESFJs. Their teacher can provide a bridge by arranging concrete learning experiences first in any learning sequence, before using the textbook. They do expect to be held accountable for understanding specific abstractions, and they want to know just what is expected of them. They do their best work when they clearly see the practical, here-and-now usefulness of assignments. They like tasks that require observation of specifics and their memory of facts. They rely a lot on their knack for memorizing. But things that are memorized are likely to be lost unless they become meaningful in practical use. Being naturally observant of details in the here and now, they tend to overlook the big picture and general meanings. They prefer teachers and textbooks that help them stay in touch with the key points by using illustrations, summaries, and examples.

Mental processing. ESFJs describe their minds as a continuous flow of facts and impressions, a reviewing of their past experiences, particularly about relationships with people. They review the past experiences to extract rules-of-thumb to guide their present lives. They prefer to solve problems by weighing value issues in the context of deeply held beliefs and personal priorities. They want to make decisions that take into account other people's needs and concerns, and they are wary of impersonal reasoning and arguments that do not attend adequately to feelings. They want to find harmonious solutions to problems, to bring people along by showing appreciation and interest in them. They tend to tackle impersonal problems by converting them into personal ones so that they can use their people skills in solving them.

INFP Learning Style

For INFPs, the best learning comes when they are quietly absorbed in pursuing ideas they care about, and seeing possibilities and connections. They are naturally curious about almost anything that engages their imagination. Their curiosity often takes them into a wide range of interests that they explore in their own individual, private way. They are very sensitive to their environment and explore it tentatively until they feel secure in it. This includes the classroom environment, where they can be highly energized when they feel support and drained when they feel abrasiveness. Although they are open-minded and adaptable, they will have a very hard time cooperating with any teacher who seems unfair or uncaring to students.

Individual and private. For INFPs learning is an individual and private matter. They usually prefer to teach themselves whatever they believe they need to know, but are willing to have the teacher make a contribution too. As means of individual learning, reading and writing are important to INFPs. They enjoy words. Being curious readers, they like individual learning assignments that put them on their own initiative and give them opportunities for self-instruction and self-expression. They also look for opportunities to be creative and original. In their writing they like metaphorical language and mind-mapping.

Relationship with teachers. INFPs care about pleasing their teacher, and they appreciate individual coaching the teacher gives them—so long as they don't feel singled out in front of others. Being naturally self-critical, INFPs may feel very hurt by teacher feedback that seems to heap still more criticism on them. The teacher will be more successful by listening carefully to find out what the INFP is trying to do and then coaching with concrete suggestions. Grades and rewards a teacher may give are not nearly as important as the quality of the relationship with the teacher or as the INFPs' own sense of satisfaction with their work.

Mental processing. INFPs describe their minds as a continuous flow of ideas and imaginings—about experiences, particularly about relationships and human value issues—with all the ideas related to each other in complex ways. Their kind of mind is quick in seeing associations and meanings, reading between the lines, and grasping general concepts. They enjoy finding broad meanings without attending to all the details. Concentrating on general meanings, they run the risk of overlooking details and practical matters. They rely on insight more than on careful observation of details, and on language skills more than on their memory of facts. They will enjoy and remember facts if they have personal meanings attached to them. Their kind of mind is organized in sets of personal values and priorities. New things are learned as they are seen as important in this personal system. Their reasoning process being based on person-oriented values, they prefer to solve problems by weighing value issues in the context of their deeply-held beliefs and personal priorities. They are wary of impersonal reasoning and arguments that do not attend adequately to feelings and key human values. INFPs pursue ideals, for themselves and others, and these give focus and energy to their work. They often use writing as a way to express their ideals.

Conceptual learning. INFPs naturally start any learning task trying to find the big picture and key concepts, looking for connections to their important values. Teachers will be most effective with them when they call attention to the context and broad meanings first before beginning to focus on skills, facts, and specifics. They like to find their own way through new material as opposed to following linear, step by step, preplanned processes provided by the teacher or textbook.

Study style. The INFP study style is spontaneous, flowing with surges of energy toward whatever pulls their curiosity. Their open and exploring approach to learning does not fit easily within set plans and schedules. They have many interests competing for their immediate attention. They find it hard to predict when the impulse will come to focus on a particular assignment. Because they want to go deeply into what interests them, they will study with great energy and concentration when their learning assignments coincide with their interests. When they must learn material that seems foreign or less important, they can handle it by finding an angle from which to see it as enhancing one of their priority values. When they develop this kind of self- discipline, INFPs teach themselves how to fit into institutional schedules.

Instruction. INFPs appreciate systematically organized instruction, but they want it to allow for individual work they can do in their own way. In high school and beyond, they generally like well organized lectures from teachers they respect. They usually do well with assignments that provide for low structure and inductive exploration. They like to invent their own ways to solve problems, and enjoy independent study. Unless INFPs have some real choices in the ways they work out their assignments, they may feel quite cramped. A system of individual agreements between teacher and students, in which students can negotiate some activities, is a plan INFPs can support and enjoy. They do their best work when it feels like play. But because learning is a private matter for them, the play may be mental play that doesn't involve other people.

ISFP Learning Style

For ISFPs, the best learning comes when they are quietly absorbed in sensory-rich activities. They are naturally curious about almost anything that engages their senses. The curiosity often takes them into physically exploring many things in their own individual, private way. They are very sensitive to their environment and explore it tentatively until they feel secure in it. This includes the classroom environment, where they can be highly energized when they feel support and drained when they feel abrasiveness. Although they are open-minded and adaptable, they will find it very hard to cooperate with any teacher who seems unfair or uncaring to students.

Sensory learning. They learn mainly through their senses, doing best with instruction that allows them to hear and touch as well as see what they are learning. They like films, audio-visual presentations, labs, materials that can be handled, computer-assisted instruction, examples, demonstrations and especially first-hand experience that gives practice in the skills and concepts to be learned. Reading, which engages only the sense of sight, is not the way of learning about new things that ISFP children prefer, but they can master reading and enjoy it, especially if it is taught in concrete, step-by-step ways. When they are confident in their ability to read, they appreciate the efficiency it brings as a learning tool.

Learning is a private matter. ISFPs prefer to work individually. They do not generally like independent study, preferring to work individually within the framework prescribed by the teacher. ISFPs care about pleasing their teacher, and they appreciate individual coaching the teacher gives them—so long as they don't feel singled out in front of others. Being naturally self-critical, ISFPs may feel very hurt by teacher feedback that seems to heap still more criticism on them. The teacher will be more successful by listening carefully to find out what the ISFP is trying to do and then coaching with concrete suggestions. Many young ISFPs are not likely to ask the teacher for help, even when they want and need it. They like a system of instruction with monitoring and feedback built in.

Mental processing. ISFPs describe their minds as organized in sets of personal values rather than in logical, objective categories. They prefer to solve problems by sifting through value issues rather than by objective analysis. They look to others for analytical reasoning and contribute to others their acute awareness of people's values and personal relationship issues.

Study style. The ISFP study style is spontaneous, flowing with surges of impulsive energy toward whatever pulls their curiosity. Their open and exploring approach to learning does not fit easily within set plans and schedules. They find it hard to predict when the impulse to study will come. Because they want to go deeply into what interests them, they will study with great energy and concentration when their learning assignments coincide with their interests. Developing this kind of self discipline, ISFPs teach themselves how to fit into institutional schedules.

Their own pace. ISFPs want ample time for quiet mental processing, and dislike being rushed. They get frustrated with a teacher who moves too quickly through material, touching just the high spots or jumping from thought to thought. They do not want to be required to fill in the gaps with their intuition. Being naturally observant of details in the here and now, they may overlook the big picture and general meanings.

Practical purposes. They do their best work when they clearly see the practical, here-and-now usefulness of assignments. They like tasks that require observation of specifics and memory of facts. They rely a lot on their knack for memorizing. But things that are memorized are likely to be lost unless they become meaningful through practical use.

Instruction. ISFPs value instruction that emphasizes informal problem solving, in contrast to the preplanned structure of most textbooks and teaching methods. They are at their best when the instruction calls for them to manage emerging problems, as in laboratory work. They do well with assignments that provide structured, hands-on exploratory observation—in contrast to open-ended inductive discovery. They like to invent their own ways to solve problems. Unless ISFPs have some real choices in the ways they work out their assignments, they may feel invaded. They like a system of individual contracts between teacher and students, in which students can negotiate some activities. They also like to take a playful approach to their work, and do their best work when it feels like play.

ESTP learning style

For ESTPs, the best learning comes when they are absorbed in sensory-rich, physical activities. They are naturally curious about almost anything that engages their senses. As children, they want to touch everything. Their curiosity often takes them into physically exploring, at least briefly, many things the teacher or parent did not have in mind for them. Although they are easy-going and adaptable, they find it very hard to study for a teacher who expects children to sit quietly and limits instruction mainly to textbooks, worksheets, and recitation. They feel the pull of many interests besides school. Throughout life they want to try things, have new experiences, get into fresh material.

Sensory, active learning. Because they rely so much on their senses, they like to learn through television, films, audio-visual presentations, materials that can be handled, and especially first-hand experience that gives practice in the skills and concepts to be learned. Reading, which engages only the sense of sight, is not their preferred way of learning about new things, but they can master reading and enjoy it, especially if it is taught in multi-sensory and social ways, and as an interesting code to be broken. Their natural way to go about learning is through physical, whole-body activity. They like active learning opportunities such as working with a friend, activities outside the school that show them "how things really are," and student-led presentations. ESTPs like to talk, to "think out loud." They often say they do their best thinking when they are talking—their thoughts become clear as they speak them.

Logical reasoning. ESTPs do best on learning tasks that use their ability to observe specifics and remember them. They rely a lot on their knack for memorizing. They naturally take an analytical, problem solving approach to life. They say they do their best work when they feel free of emotional concerns, and they like learning situations that let them work that way. They want things to be logical, to make sense in logical ways, and they resist explanations or assignments that aren't.

Study style. When studying subjects they care about, they go carefully and thoroughly through the material, wanting to have their understanding be sound and accurate. They want to have their facts straight and logically organized. Their minds like to build knowledge step by step, even though their interest and energy move impulsively rather than in a steady flow. They get frustrated with the teacher who moves too quickly through material, touching on just abstract ideas or jumping from thought to thought. They do their best work when their learning assignments clearly connect with the practical realities of their present lives, and they learn principles and theories by extracting them from their own concrete experiences. They do not envision themselves very far in the future, so studying something because "someday you'll need it" is not a meaningful reason. They learn what is useful for their present interests.

Spontaneous learning. The ESTP study style is spontaneous, flowing with surges of impulsive energy toward whatever pulls their curiosity. Their open and exploring approach to learning does not fit easily within set plans and schedules. They find it hard to predict when the impulse to study will come, but they can learn to go deeply into some interests, postpone other interests, and block out distractions. Developing this kind of self discipline, ESTPs teach themselves how to fit into institutional schedules. Sometimes, serious external deadlines are needed to dictate which interest must be given top priority. When they have assignments that make sense to them, they can apply their best energy and talent.

Instruction that fits. ESTPs value instruction that emphasizes informal problem solving, in contrast to the preplanned structure of most textbooks and teaching methods. They are at their best when the instruction calls for them to manage emerging problems, as in some educational games and laboratory work. They like to learn by constructing things and responding to problems that show up in the process. ESTPs enjoy the role of the resourceful, adaptable problem solver. They do well with assignments that provide structured, hands-on exploratory observation—in contrast to open-ended inductive discovery. They like to use their own ways of solving problems. Unless ESTPs have some real choices in the ways they work out their assignments, they may feel imprisoned. A system of individual contracts between teacher and students, in which students can negotiate some activities, is a plan ESTPs can support and enjoy. They like to take a playful approach to their work, and do their best work when it feels like play.

ESFP learning style

For ESFPs, the best learning comes when they are absorbed in sensory-rich, physical activities. They are naturally curious about almost anything that engages their senses, especially people. As children, they want to touch everything. Their curiosity often takes them into physically exploring, at least briefly, many things the teacher or parent did not have in mind for them. Although they are easy-going and adaptable, they find it very hard to study for a teacher who expects children to sit quietly and limits instruction mainly to textbooks, worksheets, and recitation. They feel the pull of many interests besides school work. Throughout life they want to try things, have new experiences, get into fresh material.

Sensory learning. Because they rely so much on their senses, they like to learn through television, films, audio-visuals, materials that can be handled, and especially first-hand experience that gives practice in the skills and concepts to be learned. Reading, which engages only the sense of sight, is not their preferred way of learning about new things, but they can master reading and enjoy it, especially if it is taught in multi-sensory and social ways, and as an interesting code to be broken. Their natural way to go about learning is through physical, whole-body learning.

Personal learning. ESFPs like to learn through relationships; for example, one-to-one with the teacher, discussions, studying with a friend, activities outside the classroom involving people, student-led presentations, and tutoring a student. ESFPs like to talk, and they value these kinds of opportunities to "think out loud." They often say they do their best thinking when talking—their thoughts become clear as they speak them. Being sociable, they can benefit a lot from having friends who value studying. They prefer to solve problems by sifting through value issues rather than by impersonal analysis. They look to others for analytical reasoning and contribute to others their acute awareness of personal relationship issues.

Study style. ESFPs do best on learning tasks that use their ability to observe specifics and remember them. They rely a lot on their knack for memorizing. When studying subjects they care about, they go carefully and thoroughly through the material, wanting to have their understanding be sound and accurate. Their minds like to build knowledge step by step, even though their interest and energy move impulsively rather than in a steady flow. They get frustrated with the teacher who moves too quickly through material, touching on just the abstract ideas or jumping from thought to thought. They do their best work when assignments clearly connect with the practical realities of their present lives, and they learn principles and theories by extracting them from their own concrete experiences. They do not envision themselves very far in the future, so studying something because "someday you'll need it" is not a meaningful reason. They learn what is useful for their present interests.

Spontaneous learning. The ESFP study style is spontaneous, flowing with surges of impulsive energy toward whatever pulls their curiosity. Their open and exploring approach to learning does not fit easily within set plans and schedules. They find it hard to predict when the impulse to study will come, but they can learn to go deeply into some interests, postpone other interests, and block out distractions. Developing this kind of self discipline, ESFPs teach themselves how to fit into institutional schedules. When they have assignments that have practical value and they care about, they can bring their best energy and talent to the task.. Those assignments they are much more likely to carry to the finish line.

Problem solving. ESFPs value instruction that emphasizes informal problem solving, in contrast to the preplanned structure of most textbooks and teaching methods. They are at their best when the instruction calls for them to manage emerging problems, as in some educational games and laboratory work. They do well with assignments that provide structured, hands-on exploratory observation—in contrast to open-ended inductive discovery. They like to invent their own ways to solve problems. Unless ESFPs have some real choices in the ways they work out their assignments, they may feel imprisoned. A system of individual contracts between teacher and students, in which students can negotiate some activities, is a plan ESFPs can support and enjoy. They do their best work when it feels like play.

Learning from a teacher. They like individual relationships with teachers, and want personal feedback from them. ENFPs feel drained by disapproval, but energized by supportive feedback. They expect to like or respect the teacher, but the teacher can quickly earn their disrespect if they believe the teacher is not treating students fairly. If they do not have respect or liking for the teacher, it is very hard for them to learn well in that classroom.

ISTJ learning style

For ISTJs, the best learning happens when they are quietly absorbed in observing and organizing their experiences to pull out the facts they need to remember. School learning is serious work for ISTJs. They want to be shown exactly what is expected of them and do not want to waste time discovering it for themselves. During school years, they think of knowledge as something that objectively exists (not something to be created), and learning is for the purpose of mastering it. They believe that careers require specific skills and facts they should master before they can be competent and make contributions to the world.

Clear, sensory instruction. For ISTJs to learn best, they first want to have a clear statement of what the instruction is about; then to see (and hear and touch, if possible) an example and demonstration of what is to be learned; then have guided practice until no more help is needed. Often they are helped by relevant, good quality audio-visual presentations, labs, materials that can be handled, and computer-assisted instruction, but first-hand, concrete experience is best.

Concrete processes. They learn abstract principles and concepts best by extracting them out of concrete experience, especially their own direct experience. Most textbooks, especially beyond the elementary school, present abstractions first, followed (sometimes) by concrete examples. This sequence runs against the thought processes of ISTJs. Their teacher can provide a bridge by arranging concrete learning experiences first in any learning sequence, before using the textbook.

Reading, which engages only the sense of sight, may not be their first choice of ways to learn about new things. ISTJ children can and do enjoy reading if they are taught it correctly, step by step, as a code that is interesting to break. When they are confident in their ability to read, they appreciate the efficiency it brings as a learning tool. They want reading material that has a clear, straight-forward presentation, beginning-middle-end, and a lot more concrete facts than generalizations or ambiguities.

Learning is a private matter. After the teacher introduces new material, and they know what to do, ISTJs would rather work alone. New information is harder to absorb in group work. They do not generally choose independent, exploratory study, preferring the efficiency of working individually within the framework prescribed by the teacher.

Goal oriented. ISTJs want their goals clearly in mind as they work. Goals and schedules planned at the beginning help them feel free to concentrate on the specifics of the task. They draw energy from the steady, orderly process of working, taking pleasure from each small completion as they move toward the end of the job. They like milestones, markers to acknowledge completions.

Careful, detailed learning. They want to work carefully and thoroughly, always aiming for soundness of understanding. They go step by step through new material so as to grasp it soundly. ISTJs dislike being rushed, and want ample time for quiet mental processing. They get frustrated with the teacher who moves too quickly through material, touching just the high spots or jumping from thought to thought. They do not want to be required to fill in the gaps with their intuition, their least-favored mental process. Being naturally observant of details in the here and now, they tend to overlook the big picture and general meanings. They prefer teachers and textbooks that help them stay in touch with the key points by using illustrations, graphs, tables, and summaries.

Practical purposes. They do their best work when they clearly see the practical, here-and-now usefulness of assignments. They like tasks that require observations of specifics and their memory of facts. They rely a lot on their knack for memorizing. ISTJs especially enjoy pulling up a stored fact for a particular purpose.

Factual and logical minded. ISTJs usually describe their minds as a continuous flow of facts and impressions, a reviewing of their past experiences that they analyze objectively and sort into logical categories. Wanting their learning activities to match these mental processes, they prefer that instruction be well structured and move in a logical and orderly way, from concrete to abstract.

ISFJ learning style

For ISFJs, the best learning happens when they are quietly absorbed in observing and organizing their experiences to pull out the facts and memories most worth keeping. School learning is serious work for ISFJs. They believe the adult world has specific skills and facts they should master. They want to be shown exactly what is expected of them and do not want to waste time discovering it for themselves.

Sensory learning. They learn mainly through their senses, doing best with instruction that allows them to hear and touch as well as see what they are learning. They want the teacher to give examples and demonstrate what is to be learned, then guide their practice until no more help is needed. Many young ISFJs are not likely to ask the teacher for help, even when they want and need it. They like a system of instruction with monitoring and feedback built in. They may be helped by relevant, good quality audio-visual presentations, labs, materials that can be handled, and computer-assisted instruction, but concrete, first-hand experience is best.

Reading, which engages only the sense of sight, may not be their first choice of ways to learn about new things. ISFJ children can and do enjoy reading if they are taught it correctly, step by step, as a code that is interesting to break. When they become confident in their ability to read, they can become avid readers.

Learning is a private matter. ISFJs prefer to study individually or with a close friend. They do not generally like independent study, preferring to work individually within the framework prescribed by the teacher. ISFJs care about pleasing their teacher, and they appreciate individual coaching the teacher gives them—so long as they don't feel singled out in front of others. They appreciate a teacher who shows caring for students, has a smooth-running and friendly classroom, and holds students accountable for their behavior and assignments.

Goal oriented. ISFJs want their goals clearly in mind as they work. Goals and schedules planned at the beginning help them feel free to concentrate on the specifics of the task. They draw energy from the steady, orderly process of working, taking pleasure from each small completion as they move toward the end of the job. They like milestones, markers to acknowledge completions.

Careful, detailed learning. They want to do their work carefully and thoroughly, always aiming for soundness of understanding. They go step by step through new material so as to grasp it soundly. ISFJs dislike being rushed, and want ample time for quiet mental processing. They get frustrated with the teacher who moves too quickly through material, touching on just the high spots or jumping from thought to thought. They do not want to be required to fill in the gaps with their intuition, their least favored mental process. Being naturally observant of details in the here and now, they tend to overlook the big picture and general meanings.

Practical purposes. They do their best work when they clearly see the practical, here-and-now usefulness of assignments. They like tasks that require observation of specifics and memory of facts. They rely a lot on their knack for memorizing, but things that are memorized are likely to be lost unless they become meaningful through practical use.

Fact and value minded. ISFJs describe their minds as a continuous flow of facts and impressions, a reviewing of their past experiences, particularly about relationships with people. They review the past experiences to extract rules-of-thumb to guide their present lives. They prefer to solve problems by sifting through value issues rather than by objective analysis. They look to others for analytical reasoning and contribute to others their acute awareness of people's values and personal relationship issues.

From concrete to abstract. ISFJs want their instruction to be formalized and to flow in an orderly way, step by step, from concrete to abstract. They learn abstract principles and concepts by distilling them out of their own personal, concrete experiences. Most textbooks, especially beyond the elementary school, present abstractions first, followed (sometimes) by concrete examples. This sequence runs against the thought processes of ISFJs. Their teacher can provide a bridge by arranging concrete learning experiences first in any learning sequence, before using the textbook.

ENTP learning style

For ENTPs, the best learning comes when they are enthusiastically pursuing a new interest. They thrive on the surge of inspiration that comes with the new interest or project. They are naturally curious about almost anything that engages their intuition, their doorway to serious learning. As children, they want to be everywhere and do everything. Their curiosity often takes them into exploring, at least briefly, many things the teacher or parent did not have in mind for them. Although they are easy-going and adaptable, they find it hard to study for a teacher who expects children to sit quietly and limits instruction mainly to textbooks, worksheets, and recitation. They feel the pull of many interests besides school. Throughout life they want to try things, have new experiences, get into fresh material.

Mental processing. ENTPs describe their minds as a continuous flow of ideas and possibilities. They construct and reconstruct mental models of their ideas, analyzing complexities and envisioning how things could be made or done. Their kind of mind is quick in seeing associations and meanings, and grasping general concepts. Concentrating on general meanings, they may overlook details and practical matters. They rely on insight more than on careful observation, and on conceptual and language skills more than on their memory of facts. They naturally take an analytical, problem solving approach to life. They say they do their best work when they feel objective and free from emotional concerns.

Interactive learning. ENTPs like learning situations that give them a chance to talk—whenever the talk includes fresh material or challenges. For example, they like one-to-one discussion with the teacher, classroom discussions that aren't recitations, studying with a friend, action projects involving people, and making oral presentations. They value these opportunities to "think out loud." They often say they do their best thinking when they are talking—their thoughts become clear as they speak them. While young ENTPs prefer interactive learning, they also value reading. They enjoy words. Being curious readers, they like learning assignments that put them on their own initiative and give them opportunities for self-instruction and self-expression. They also look for opportunities to be inventive and original.

Conceptual learning. ENTPs naturally start any learning task trying to find the big picture and key concepts, bringing into play the features of mental processing described above. Teachers will be most effective with them when they call attention to the context and broad meanings first before beginning to focus on skills, facts, and specifics. They like to find their own way through new material as opposed to following linear, step by step, preplanned processes provided by the teacher or textbook. Their energy for studying is seriously drained if such linear processes are the only ones allowed.

Study style. The ENTP study style is spontaneous, flowing with surges of energy toward whatever pulls their curiosity. Their open and exploring approach to learning does not fit easily within set plans and schedules. Many interests compete for their immediate attention. ENTPs tend to keep a lot of interests on their plate all the time, shifting their focus from one to another. They find it hard to predict when the impulse to focus on a particular learning assignment will come. Sometimes, serious external deadlines are needed to dictate which interest must be given top priority. However, they can learn to go deeply into some interests, postpone or discard other interests, and minimize distractions. Developing this kind of self discipline, ENTPs teach themselves how to fit into institutional schedules.

Beginnings are a lot more important than endings to ENTPs, because beginnings are fired with the fascination of new possibilities. When they have study assignments they can feel enthusiastic about, they are much more likely to carry them to the finish line. Unless ENTPs have some real choices in the ways they work out their assignments, they may feel very cramped. They do well with a system of individual contracts between teacher and students, in which students can negotiate some learning activities involving interests that spark their enthusiasm.

Informal problem solving. ENTPs value instruction that emphasizes informal problem solving, in contrast to the preplanned structure of most textbooks and teaching methods. In high school and beyond, they generally like well organized and competent lectures, but with time reserved for other kinds of learning as well. They are at their best when the instruction calls for them to manage emerging problems, as in some educational games and laboratory and computer work. They do well with assignments that provide low structure and inductive exploration. They like to find their own way through new material and invent their own ways to solve problems. They also do their best work when it feels like play.

ENFP learning style

For ENFPs, the best learning comes when they are enthusiastically pursuing a new interest. They thrive on feeling inspired. They are naturally curious about almost anything that engages their imagination, their doorway to serious learning. As children, they want to be everywhere and do everything. Their curiosity often takes them into exploring, at least briefly, many things the teacher or parent did not have in mind. Although they are easy-going and adaptable, they find it very hard to study for a teacher who expects children to sit quietly and limits instruction mainly to textbooks, worksheets, and recitation. They feel the pull of many interests besides school work. Throughout life they want to try things and have new experiences.

Interactive learning. ENFPs like to learn through personal relationships; for example, one-to-one with the teacher, classroom discussions with a lot of flow between students and teacher, studying with a friend, action projects involving people, idea discussions in a group, making oral presentations, and tutoring other students. As adults, they usually enjoy having a mentor to guide their learning. ENFPs like to talk, and they value these kinds of opportunities to "think out loud." They often say they do their best thinking when they are talking—their thoughts become clear as they speak them.

Mental processing. ENFPs describe their minds as a continuous flow of ideas and imaginings—about experiences, particularly about relationships with people. Their kind of mind is quick in seeing associations and meanings, reading between the lines, and grasping general concepts. Concentrating on general meanings, they may overlook specifics and practical matters. They rely on insight more than on careful observation, and on their language skills more than on their memory of facts. They will enjoy and remember facts if they have personal meanings attached to them. Facts are gathered to have enough information to sell an idea to somebody. Their kind of mind is organized in sets of personal values and priorities. New things are learned as they are seen as important in this personal system.

Conceptual learning. ENFPs naturally start any learning task trying to find the big picture and key concepts. Teachers will be most effective with them when they call attention to the context and broad meanings first before beginning to focus on skills, facts, and specifics. They like to find their own way through new material as opposed to following linear, step by step, preplanned processes provided by the teacher or textbook. Reading and writing are important ways of learning for ENFPs. They enjoy words. Being curious readers, they like learning assignments that put them on their own initiative and give them opportunities for self-instruction and self-expression. They also look for opportunities to be creative and original. In their writing they like metaphorical language and mind-mapping.

Study style. The ENFP study style is spontaneous, flowing with surges of energy toward whatever pulls their curiosity. Their open and exploring approach to learning does not fit easily within set plans and schedules. Their way of dealing with required assignments has been described as "put it off - cram - pull it off." They find it hard to predict when the impulse to focus on a particular assignment will come, but they can learn to go deeply into some interests, postpone other interests, and minimize distractions. Developing this kind of self discipline, ENFPs teach themselves how to fit into institutional schedules. They like beginnings a lot more than endings, because beginnings are fired with the fascination of new possibilities. When they have study assignments they can feel enthusiastic about, they are much more likely to carry them to the finish line.

Informal problem solving. ENFPs value instruction that emphasizes informal problem solving—brainstorming, sharing possibilities with others, finding or inventing a way through a problem—in contrast to the preplanned structure of most textbooks and teaching methods. In high school and beyond, they generally like well organized lectures, but with time reserved for other kinds of learning as well. They are at their best when excited about ideas and when dealing with problems as they emerge. They often like to invent their own ways to solve problems. Unless ENFPs have some real choices in the ways they work out their assignments, they may feel cramped. They do well with a system of individual contracts between teacher and students, in which students can negotiate some activities. They do their best work when they see it as fun.

Learning from a teacher. They care about maintaining individual relationships with teachers, and very much want personal feedback from them. ENFPs feel drained down by disapproval, but energized by supportive feedback. They expect to like or respect the teacher, but the teacher can quickly earn their disrespect if they believe the teacher is not treating students fairly. If they do not have respect or liking for the teacher, they are less likely to learn well in that classroom.

INTJ learning style

For INTJs, the best learning comes when they are quietly absorbed in pursuing new ideas and possibilities. They thrive on the surge of inspiration that comes with the new idea or interest. They are naturally curious about almost anything that engages their imagination, and they explore their interests in their own individual, private way. They take the long view and are focused on the future more than the present.

Independent and private. Highly independent, they often prefer to teach themselves whatever they believe they need to know, but they also appreciate the contributions of a teacher they regard as competent. Their learning is a private matter. Reading is one of their main ways of learning. Being avid readers, they like self-instruction, independent study, and learning assignments that put them on their own initiative. They dislike most kinds of group work in school, and they like to find their own way through new material. They also look for opportunities to be inventive and original. They like their processes and results to be innovative and distinctive. They set high standards for their work, push themselves hard, and are self-critical when their results do not meet their expectations.

Mental processing. INTJs describe their minds as a continuous flow of ideas. They construct and reconstruct mental models of their ideas, envisioning how things could be made or done. Their kind of mind is quick in seeing associations and meanings, reading between the lines, and grasping general concepts. They put a high value on intellectual quickness.

Many meanings come to them when their conscious mind is focused on something else. Some of their best problem solving comes out of unconscious processing, where ideas have been "cooking on the back burner." They are likely to be most effective when they allow time for that process to happen.

Insight. INTJs place a high value on insight. Insights grasped by their intuition seem simultaneously certain, clear, simple, and complex. Of course, it is important for INTJs to test the soundness of their insights with external facts—which is usually hard to do because the appeal of the inner vision makes facts seem puny or irrelevant in comparison. They rely on insight more than on careful observation, and on conceptual and language skills more than on their memory of facts. Concentrating on general meanings, they run the risk of overlooking details and practical matters.

Critical thinking. INTJs naturally take a detached, analytical, and skeptical approach to issues and problems. They see complexities and enjoy probing them. Their approach to improving themselves and others is by pointing out flaws, a tendency that sometimes is not appreciated by others. Wanting to stay cool as they work through problems, they say their minds work best when they feel free from the distractions of emotional concerns, and they like learning situations that let them work that way.

Competence and mastery. These are important to INTJs. They believe competence comes through inspiration, insight, and analytical thinking. Sometimes the surge of inspiration that energizes their learning is brought up short by the reality of having to master essentials that aren't inspiring. Many times they have to push themselves to get interested in learning some "essentials" because their goal of mastery takes priority in that situation.

Structure and closure. INTJs want to map out a clear plan as they work. Goals and schedules planned at the beginning help them feel free to concentrate on the tasks they need to do. They draw energy from moving through their schedule, taking pleasure from the completions that move them toward the end of the job. They like milestones, markers to acknowledge completions.

Organized instruction. They like instruction to be systematically organized, including teacher lectures. They usually are not tolerant of the teacher who does not present things logically. Because logical analysis is their own main way of reasoning, they prefer teachers who reason as they do and give them challenging analytical problems to work on. Their minds, governed by intuition, do not take in information in a detailed, step by step way, and INTJs generally are not patient with instruction designed in that way. They like the teacher who presents the big picture even if missing some steps or details may hinder them later.

INFJ learning style

For INFJs, the best learning comes when they are quietly absorbed in pursuing new ideas and possibilities. They thrive on the surge of inspiration that comes with the new idea or interest. They are naturally curious about almost anything that engages their imagination, and they explore their interests in their own individual, private way. Their interests are mostly in planning ways for helping improve people's lives. They take the long view, and are focused on the future.

Individual and private. Highly independent, they usually prefer to teach themselves whatever they believe they need to know, but are willing to have the teacher make a contribution too. They care about maintaining good relationships with their teachers, valuing highly the teachers' feedback about them, but they always protect their independence. Their learning is a private matter. Reading is one of their main ways of learning. Being avid readers, they like self-instruction, independent study, and learning assignments that put them on their own initiative. They like to find their own way through new material. They set high standards for their work, and push themselves hard. They like their results to be innovative and distinctive.

Mental processing. INFJs describe their minds as a continuous flow of ideas, all related to each other in complex ways. Their kind of mind is quick in seeing associations and meanings, reading between the lines, and grasping general concepts. Many meanings come to them when their conscious mind is focused on something else. Some of their best problem solving comes when they allow time for unconscious processing, having ideas "cooking on the back burner."

Insight. INFJs place a high value on insight. Insights grasped by their intuition seem simultaneously certain, clear, simple, and complex. Of course, it is important for INFJs to test the soundness of their insights with external facts—which is usually hard to do because the appeal of the inner vision makes facts seem puny or irrelevant in comparison. They rely on insight more than on careful observation, and on language skills more than on their memory of facts. Concentrating on general meanings, they run the risk of overlooking details and practical matters.

Problem Solving. Their reasoning process is based on person-oriented values. They prefer to solve problems by weighing value issues in the context of deeply held beliefs and personal priorities. They want to make decisions that take into account other people's needs and concerns, and they are wary of impersonal reasoning and arguments that do not attend adequately to feelings. They want to find harmonious solutions to problems, to bring people along by showing appreciation and interest in them.

Idealistic. INFJs pursue ideals, for themselves and others. They are most energized when their intuition shows them ideals that can give form and direction to their work. They often use writing as a way of expressing their ideals. They may idealize people they respect and care about. They will work harder for a teacher they idealize and may have their motivation crash when such a teacher fails to live up to the ideal. Maturing as an INFJ means, in part, learning how to move on from such disappointments and kindle interest again in the things that are important.

Goal oriented. INFJs want their goals clearly in mind as they work. Goals planned at the beginning help them feel free to concentrate and effectively use their creative energies. They want opportunities to be creative and original, and can do that best when they have choices in the ways they work toward their goals. They also draw energy from the orderly process of doing their work, taking pleasure from each small completion as they move toward the end of the job. Sometimes, being creative is not orderly and it interferes with keeping a schedule. The conflict between the two may cause stress in the INFJ.

Favored instruction. INFJs respond best to a teacher who is even-handed and respectful of students. In high school and beyond, they usually like a lecture-style presentation because it lets them concentrate on the subject without concern for maintaining relationships in group-style learning activities. Their minds, governed by intuition, do not take in information in a detailed, step by step way. They like the teacher who presents the big picture and broad expectations and then lets them go around or beyond the standard ways, even if missing some steps or details may hinder them later. With high expectations for themselves, INFJs often are very self-critical. Because of their self-criticism, they may feel very hurt by teacher feedback that seems to heap still more criticism on them. The teacher will be more successful by taking care in finding out what the INFJ is trying to do and then coaching with suggestions.

Further Resources

Discovering Learning Preferences and Learning Differences in the Classroom by June R. Bargar, Robert R. Bargar, Jamie M. Cano. Columbus, OH: Ohio Agricultural Education Curriculum Materials Service, Ohio State University, 1994.

Effective Teaching, Effective Learning: Making the Personality Connection in Your Classroom by Alice M. Fairhurst and Lisa L. Fairhurst. Palo Alto, CA: Davies-Black Publishing, 1995.

Gifts Differing by Isabel Myers with Peter B. Myers. Palo Alto, CA: Consulting Psychologists Press, 1980.

Introduction to Type in College by John K. DiTiberio and Allen L. Hammer. Palo Alto, CA: Consulting Psychologists Press, 1993.

Looking at Type and Careers by Charles R. Martin. Gainesville, FL: Center for Applications of Psychological Type, 1995.

Looking at Type: The Fundamentals by Charles R. Martin. Gainesville, FL: Center for Applications of Psychological Type, 1997.

Most Excellent Differences: Essays on Using Type Theory in the Composition Classroom by Thomas C. Thompson, editor. Gainesville, FL: Center for Applications of Psychological Type, 1997.

Nurture by Nature: Understand Your Child's Personality Type and Become A Better Parent by Paul D. Tieger and Barbara Barron-Tieger. Boston: Little, Brown and Company, 1997.

One of A Kind: Making the Most of Your Child's Uniqueness. Gainesville, FL: Center for Applications of Psychological Type, 1995. (Original work 1988)

People Types and Tiger Stripes (3rd edition) by Gordon D. Lawrence. Gainesville, FL: Center for Applications of Psychological Type, 1993.

Procrastination: Using Psychological Type Concepts to Help Students by Judith A. Provost. Gainesville, FL: Center for Applications of Psychological Type, 1988.

Strategies for Success: Using Type to Do Better in High School and College by Judith A. Provost. Gainesville, FL: Center for Applications of Psychological Type, 1992.

Writing and Personality: Finding Your Voice, Your Style, Your Way by John K. DiTiberio and George H. Jensen. Palo Alto, CA: Davies-Black Publishing, 1995.

Background Notes

About the Author

Gordon Lawrence is the author of *People Types and Tiger Stripes*, one of the first books about applying the concepts underlying the Myers-Briggs Type Indicator. Widely used, this book is now in its third edition. During 25 years of teaching graduate studies in education, he focused his teaching, research, and writing on ways to improve teaching and instructional leadership. He has taught thousands of people about psychological type in diverse organizations—educational, industrial, and public service.

He was the third president of the Association for Psychological Type and directed the development of its MBTI Training Program. He serves on the Board of Directors of the Center for Applications of Psychological Type. Retired from the University of Florida, Dr. Lawrence now writes, consults, and conducts training.

About the Publisher

The Center for Applications of Psychological Type, Inc. (CAPT) was established in the summer of 1975 with two major goals: to help make what is already known about psychological types useful in practical ways and to create new knowledge. Its founders, Isabel Briggs Myers and Mary H. McCaulley, adopted "the constructive use of differences" as the motto for this non-profit organization.

CAPT educates the public and professionals to view differences constructively by maintaining a number of services for use in education, counseling, organizational development, religious life, and research.

- CAPT houses the Isabel Briggs Myers Memorial Library, the largest collection of MBTI publications, dissertations, and theses in the world. Research services are also available through the Library.
- CAPT publishes and distributes papers and books related to research and practical applications of the Indicator. On-going research is conducted and made available through new products and services.
- CAPT computer scoring for the MBTI produces high-quality, professional reports. This service attracts a large number of MBTI users; it also facilitates the collection of MBTI responses, contributing significantly to original research on the study of personality.
- The Educational Department of CAPT offers basic and advanced training worldwide for managers, educators, counselors, psychotherapists, career counselors, psychologists, organizational development consultants, and religious leaders. CAPT has also sponsored and co-sponsored international conferences since 1975.

For a catalog about all these services and products, contact CAPT.
Center for Applications of Psychological Type, Inc.
2815 N.W. 13th Street, Suite 401
Gainesville, FL 32609
(800) 777-2278
E-mail: capt@capt.org
Website: http://www.capt.org